CONTENT

D0120775

Pages 5, 45 (left), 59, 60, 61, 63 (right), 158: T. Tindall Wildridge, *The Dance of Death in Painting and in Print*, 1897; pp. 43, 57 (right), 63 (left): Madalen Edgar (ed.), *Froissart's Chronicles*, 1912; p. 86: Martin A.S. Hume, *The Courtships of Queen Elizabeth*, 1898; p. 44: Harry Johnston, *Pioneers in Tropical America*, 1914; p. 87 (left): John Foxe, *Book of Martyrs*, 1860s; p. 131: Thomas Archer, *Gladstone and his Contemporaries*, 1886; pp. 144, 145: H.W. Wilson, *His Majesty the King*, 1935; p. 90 (left): *Chatterbox*, 1914; p. 56 (right): Anon., *Glen Albyn*, 1880s?; p. 100 (lower left): Easton S. Valentine, *Fifeshire*, 1910; pp. 94 (left), 100 (upper left): Sir Walter Scott, *A Legend of Montrose*, 1878; pp. 29, 87 (right), 93, 101 (bottom left): James MacKenzie, *The History of Scotland*, 1894; pp. 52, 53: Jane Porter, *Scottish Chiefs*, 1875; p. 34: *Wilson's Tales of the Borders Vol. 1*, 1848; p. 91: G. le Faure, *La Guerre sous l'eau*, 1898; p. 22, 127 (upper right): William J. Forster, *Famous Britons*, 1903; pp. 25, 79, 89, 90 (right), 104, 148: J. Edward Parrott, *Britain Overseas*, 1908; pp. 132, 133: *The Illustrated London News*, 1849; p. 114: Allan Fea, *Some Beauties of the Seventeenth Century*, 1906; p. 12, *The Quiver*, 1888; p. 125 (right): William O'Connor Morris, *Napoleon*, 1901. The image on p. 135 is from Wikipedia Commons. The photographs on pages 51 (right), 110, 115, 116 and 118 are by the author. As ever, thanks to Ségolène Dupuy. All other images have been provided by The History Press, or come from the Library of Congress (LOC).

INTRODUCTION

This sanguinary canter through British history commences with cannibalism from the depths of prehistory and ends with the Gestapo's detailed plans for ensuring compliance once Hitler's Nazis had occupied the country. Along the way you will encounter bloodthirsty (and bloody-minded) Romans, Picts, Anglo-Saxons, Vikings, Normans, Plantagenets, Tudors and Stuarts, not to mention a rogues' gallery of murderers, pirates, assassins and military nutjobs. You will also learn the technique of blinding your enemy during a windy medieval sea battle, how to interpret the Wars of the Roses as a football match, and the use of cheese as an instrument of torture.

There are battles a-plenty in this book, for battles have traditionally provided the hooks on which to drape the greater tapestry of history.

Battles are also nice, straightforward narrative events that we can easily understand: two sides fight, one wins (usually). But battles are actually comparatively rare in the overall history of warfare. For a battle to take place, both sides must 'agree' to fight; that is, face up to each other on a certain piece of ground. But battles are high-risk events, and more time is usually spent evading battle, or manoeuvring your opponent into accepting battle on disadvantageous terms. Historically, most warfare has not consisted of pitched battles but of skirmishes (fights between small groups that are broken off before total destruction), raiding (small-scale short-term attacks with a specific aim in mind – perhaps to destroy an item of tactical value such as a bridge, or to take food, livestock or slaves) and sieges (surrounding and grinding down a town or fortress). The other common form of warfare, especially in the Middle Ages, is the *chevauchée*, an extended march through enemy (or neutral) territory, burning and pillaging everything in the way. William the Conqueror was a *chevauchée* master, and the tactic was standard practice for English armies in France and Scotland and Scottish armies in the North of England. The average *chevauchée* featured enough atrocities to shame an SS division, so they are rarely touched upon by popular histories, and skirmishes and raids are not generally very newsworthy – which is why battles dominate the narrative.

Numbers quoted for deaths in battle here should be treated with a pillar of salt, as most estimates fail to take into account deaths after battle – from wounds, infection, disease, starvation, ill-treatment and summary execution of prisoners. The dying doesn't stop when the main killing does.

Finally, it is worth pointing out that the main experience of most people for the majority of history was not blood, but mud. Most of our ancestors were not soldiers, kings or nobles, but workers; the people who brought in the harvest or performed repetitive tasks in a workshop or factory. This book is not, however, a history of agricultural drudgery or industrial grime: it is the *Bloody British History*.

AND SO:
THERE SHALL BE BLOOD.
ENJOY.

CANNIBALS FROM THE DAWN OF TIME

'Eating people is wrong.'

Flanders and Swann, 'The Reluctant Cannibal', 1956

Somewhere around 14,700 years ago, the vast ice sheets that had reduced Europe to an Arctic wasteland suddenly began to withdraw – perhaps over as little as five years. The small bands of humans who had survived the intensely cold period by huddling in their 'refuges' in slightly warmer Spain and southern France started to follow their game herds of reindeer and wild horse as the animals moved north over land that was now free of ice. Some of these humans crossed Doggerland – the now-submerged land bridge that once joined the British Isles to the Continent. A small group of them set up a seasonal shelter in Gough's Cave, now part of the world-famous network of caves in Somerset's Cheddar Gorge. And it was here that Britain's oldest-recorded cannibals consumed human flesh and drank liquids out of the skulls of both adults and children.

The evidence comes in the form of the bones of five people: two adults (one young and one older); two adolescents; and a child of about 3 years old. All had had the flesh stripped from their bodies and their bones cracked to extract the valuable marrow

inside. Cut marks on the bones showed that the bodies had been processed using the same stone tools and same high level of butchery skill that had been employed to cut up the animals whose bones were also found in the cave.

As well as cannibalism, the inhabitants of Gough's Cave also made drinking vessels out of skulls. Shortly after death, the heads were severed at the base of the skull. A stone lever was inserted into the mouth to break the lower jaw away from the main skull, and the jawbone then smashed open to extract the marrow. The tongue, lips, ears, cheeks and nose were cut away, the eyes pulled out, the major skull muscles were cut off and the scalp removed. Once the soft tissues covering the skull had been meticulously pared away, the bones of the face were smashed off, leaving just the bowl-like vault of the skull. The edges of this were then smoothed down, leaving a drinking vessel that could hold about two pints. What the cannibals were drinking is unknown, but it could easily have been just water (rather than, say, blood).

Starting with a severed head, a skilled hunter could probably have taken about half a day to fashion one of the skull-cups. The three skull-cups that have been identified came from the two adults and the 3-year-old child. At 14,700 years old, these Upper Paleolithic specimens are the oldest known skull-cups on the planet. The plates of the child's skull, by the way, had not yet fused, meaning it would have probably leaked.

It's not known why cannibalism was practiced at this place and time. There is no evidence of violent death on the bones of the five individuals, so perhaps they died of natural causes and, in the starvation economy of winter, their meat could not be allowed to go to waste.

Genetic studies, however, have found that very early humans – possibly as far back as 500,000 years ago – may have been cannibals as a matter of course. Research published in the journal *Science* in 2003 found that human populations around the world today carry a gene which protects them against prion diseases, which are serious diseases of the brain often caused by eating contaminated human flesh. We may all, it seems, be the descendants of cannibals.

Cheddar cliffs, where Britain's oldest recorded cannibals lived. (C-DIG-ppmsc-08152)

In Britain, cannibalism turns up in just a few cases in the later archaeological record:

- Between 2000–1000 BC: five leg bones discovered at Dorney Lake, Berkshire, found with stone tool cut marks, and signs of gnawing and being broken open for the marrow.

- Between 30 BC and AD 130: an adult's thigh-bone from Alveston Cave, Gloucestershire, split to extract the marrow. Many of the thirty-seven individuals found in the cave had suffered from deformities – which probably marked them out as 'different' or 'uncanny' – and several showed signs of violent death. The best guess at the moment is that they represent a Druidic ritual of mass human sacrifice, possibly connected with a desperate appeal to the gods during the time of the Roman Conquest.

- Cheddar Man, Britain's oldest complete human skeleton, was also found in Gough's Cave, this time in 1903. Dating to about 7150 BC, in the Mesolithic period, he was more than 7,000 years more recent than the cannibals of the Upper Paleolithic – but he had been murdered by a powerful blow to the back of his head. Was this the first evidence of an early British murder?

3500 BC

PREHISTORIC WARFARE

'An average of 70 per cent of men engaged in ancient battles were killed or wounded, whereas only 60 per cent of combatants in the bloodiest modern battles have become casualties.'

Lawrence Keeley, War Before Civilization, 1996

DATELINE: AROUND 3580–3535 BC

The young man had been running away when he was shot in the back by a flint-tipped arrow. He fell forward, crushing and smothering to death the infant he had been carrying in his panicked flight. Both were buried by falling rubble when the fortification around them was burned to the ground.

DATELINE: ABOUT 3570 BC

Fourteen people were slaughtered in the raid, most killed by arrows. One man's pelvic bone still contained the tip of the flint arrowhead that killed him.

DATELINE: BETWEEN 440–390 BC

The group of women and children – including babies – had their throats cut and were dumped unceremoniously into the hastily cut ditch of their uncompleted hill fort. The outer wall – started in a desperate attempt to provide a second line of defence against the attackers, but never finished – was then pulled down over the massacred bodies.

These are just three examples of archaeological evidence for warfare and communal violence in prehistoric Britain. They come from, respectively: the Neolithic Stepleton enclosure at Hambledon Hill in Dorset; the Wayland's Smithy burial chamber in Wiltshire (constructed about 800 years earlier than the nearby ritual complex of Stonehenge); and Fin Cop, a devastated Iron Age hill fort in Derbyshire.

These and several other examples give the lie to what was once a widely accepted generalisation: the idea that before the Roman invasion, prehistoric British society was relatively peaceful. It was once thought that Iron Age hill forts, for example, were mostly about demonstrating status and prestige rather than being actual defensive structures. In fact, it seems that, strangely enough, the immense labour required to construct a massive ditch, a bank and a wooden palisade is not about showing off to the neighbours, but about keeping out other people armed with lethal weapons: if it looks like a major defence, then it probably is designed for defence, and with good reason. The frenzied but doomed attempts to build a last-minute defensive wall at Fin Cop, and the subsequent massacre of women and children, show that the danger of attack was all too real. At Crickley Hill, near Cheltenham (Gloucestershire), more than 400 arrow points have been uncovered around the palisaded defences – arrows fired by an attacking force. And at Carn Brea, a well-defended Iron Age 'fortress' in Cornwall, a concentration of almost 1,000 arrow-heads has been found around the entrance. Both of these examples suggest sizable attacking forces and organised groups of archers. And groups of organised archers imply the mass production of bows and arrows – missile weapons more sophis-ticated than melee weapons such as clubs and axes – as well as training and a military hierarchy.

In the Wayland's Smithy example mentioned above, fourteen people were killed, eleven of them adult males. This was probably a raid or a surprise attack: Neolithic societies would have been unable to support sustained warfare. Eleven men may have represented a significant proportion of the total adult male population of the farming community in the area, and their loss may have had a terrible knock-on effect. Perhaps, following the raid,

the harvest was not gathered in, and many others in the community subsequently starved to death. One curious characteristic of the bodies found at Fin Cop is that they are all of women and children: no adult men have been found. It is speculated that the men were either all killed in a battle elsewhere, or taken away as slaves. The killing of children and babies suggests 'ethnic cleansing': the attackers did not want to merely defeat their enemies; they wanted to wipe them off the face of the earth.

In none of the cases cited above do we know who was doing the attacking, or why. Given the importance of livestock in prehistoric societies, it is likely that some of the violence was the result of cattle raids. Perhaps other conflicts were in pursuit of grain stores, or female captives, or prestige goods. The evidence of massed attacks on hill forts in the Iron Age, however, suggests something more serious, more organised, more purposeful – the acquisition of territory, perhaps, or control over mines or other valuable natural resources. Or simply ethnic hatred.

Whatever the reasons, it is clear that prehis-toric Britain was no golden age of peace, where intellectual mystics pondered the mysteries of the universe in stone circles and sacred sites – instead, it was a place where violent death was just an arrow-shot away.

INVASION! (ROMAN STYLE)

*'And so they managed to cross the river and kill
many of the natives who were taken by surprise.'*

Cassius Dio, Roman History, *early third century*

The massed British tribes watched fascinated as the
Romans on the opposite bank of the river appeared
to be engaged in some massive logistical activity.
Surely, the Britons thought, all this was preparation
for an assault – but how was the Roman army
going to cross the treacherous waters without a
bridge? The painted warriors watched and waited,
anticipating the moment when their knowledge
of their home terrain would inevitably lead to a
killing field when the invaders tried to cross the
River Medway.

Meanwhile, a short distance downstream,
a group of specially trained infantry from Batavia
(modern-day Netherlands) were swimming across
the river in full battle armour, quite unnoticed.
These Roman equivalent of SEALs crept up on the
place where the Britons had parked their chariots,
and cut the hamstrings of the horses, before
quickly withdrawing. Enraged at the loss of their
prized steeds, the Britons launched a headlong
pursuit to the east. And thus fell totally for the next
part of the Roman ruse.

'And we'll cross the river over there while the
Britons are distracted by our cunning plan.'

The overt preparations for crossing the river had just been a piece of theatre. While the Britons were being distracted by the withdrawing Batavians, the main Roman force was crossing the river at a narrower point upstream, to the west. The Roman commander, Aulus Plautius, had planned well. Two legions forged a bridgehead on the northern bank of the river, fighting off a British force that had not only been taken by surprise, but was lacking the tactical advantage normally supplied by their fast, agile chariots. A third legion crossed the river under cover of darkness, and now the Roman force was sufficiently strong enough to make a breakout.

Just after dawn, the Britons attacked – their total numbers are unknown, but there may have been anything up to 17,000 warriors present. Highly trained in this form of combat, the disciplined Romans pushed wedge-shaped columns into the scrum.

It was a desperate, brutal struggle that could have gone either way. After much slaughter, one legion broke out and circled back on the Britons from behind, a manoeuvre that almost cost the legion's commander, Hosidius Geta, his life. Geta, however, fighting ferociously in the midst of the combat, cut his way free, and was later honoured as a war hero back in Rome.

Encircled and 'outgunned', the Britons realised they were defeated and withdrew, leaving perhaps 5,000 dead on the battlefield. The Romans had lost around 850 men. It was the summer of AD 43, just a short time after the Roman invasion fleet had landed, and the Battle of the Medway signalled the start of the complete conquest of lowland England.

Most warfare consists of avoiding battle until the time is right, and in this sense the British leaders, the brothers Caratacus and Togodumnus, were masters of battle tactics. The landing of the invasion fleet at the north-eastern tip of Kent was unopposed because the Britons did not have enough forces in the area. The Britons gave ground and sent out small harassing units to nip at the flanks of the four legions as they moved through Kent, the skirmishes being enough to delay the Roman advance long enough for the British warriors to be gathered at a strong point – in this case on the north bank of the River Medway, somewhere to the west of modern-day Rochester. Unfortunately the Britons had severely underestimated the sheer military skill of the Romans, who had used the river-crossing ruse on previous campaigns in Europe, and had in place their Batavians as 'special forces'. The strength and tenacity of the British opposition can be judged by the fact that the fighting lasted for two days, whereas most battles of the period were over in a matter of hours.

The Britons withdrew to the north bank of the Thames, and once the Romans had (with difficulty) crossed that river, they 'slaughtered many of them', according to the Roman historian Cassius Dio. Dio goes on to state: 'But, as they [the Romans] followed up the remainder without due care, they became entangled in the trackless marshland and lost many men.'

Around this time Togodumnus died, possibly from wounds received at Medway, but his brother Caratacus carried on the fight, fleeing west and north to tribes unknown to him. Probably though a combination of support from the Druids – who may have seen in him the only military leader capable of mounting an effective resistance to the invaders – and his own personality, Caratacus mounted a fierce upland campaign that only came to an end when he was handed over to the Romans by another tribe, the Brigantes, in AD 51.

In the short term, Aulus Plautius was forced to cool his heels at the Thames while he waited, under orders, for the Emperor Claudius to arrive and 'take' the native capital of Camulodunum (Colchester) in what was nothing more than a public relations exercise designed to impress the Senate and public of Rome. With the Claudian circus taking six weeks to arrive – an imperial entourage and a troupe of war elephants do not move nimbly – Plautius, champing at the bit to

Caratacus pleading for his life before the Romans. He survived, but spent the rest of his life a captive of Rome.

consolidate the invasion, ordered the Second Augustan Legion under Vespasian to attack the south-west. Vespasian sailed to the Dorset and Hampshire coast and, according to the Roman historian Suetonius, fought thirty battles, defeated two tribes, overran the Isle of Wight and overcame twenty native fortresses. An example of Roman tactics can be found at Hod Hill, a hill fort near Blandford Forum in Dorset. There, fifteen ballista bolts were found – a ballista being a catapult that fired heavy iron-tipped arrows, a kind of Roman guided missile that could also be used to set fire to thatch and wooden buildings. The concentration of the bolts at Hod Hill suggested these artillery weapons had been mounted on a tall siege tower; from this vantage point the bolts rained down on the chieftain's hut, a tactic which led to a rapid surrender. Shock and awe.

AD 60

BURN LONDINIUM TO THE GROUND!

'On this ground we must either conquer or die with glory. There is no alternative.'

Speech attributed to Queen Boudicca (invented by Tacitus)

The IX Legion was on a forced march through eastern England. A few days earlier, it had been summoned from its winter quarters on the River Trent with the almost unbelievable news that the great city of Camulodunam (Colchester), the gleaming beacon of Roman life and civilisation in the province of Britannia, was now nothing but a fiery graveyard, its great temple toppled, its inhabitants slaughtered down to the last babe in arms.

Somewhere near Camulodunam, the IX encountered the people responsible for the conflagration: a 'rabble' of native Britons armed mostly with agricultural tools and hunting bows, their bladed weapons (such as swords) having been confiscated several years earlier. Unable to form into their defensive squares, the long column of Roman infantry found itself split up into small groups. They were annihilated. Perhaps some 2,000 men were slaughtered where they stood. The 400 or 500 cavalry, including the legion commander Petilius Cerealis, only survived by galloping away, very very fast.

The destruction of the IX Legion was a shocking blow to Roman prestige. Worse was to come. The important trading centre on the Thames, Londinium, was in the rebels' sights. With insufficient troops to defend it, the Roman military abandoned the town. The rich fled to Gaul (France) on ships. About half the city's population of 30,000 took to the roads south, refugees struggling to keep up with the troops and supply wagons as they headed for the safety of pro-Roman Kent. Those who were left behind were utterly defenceless; all were killed when the British hordes descended on the city, many being crucified, mutilated or impaled on stakes. Londinium itself became nothing more than a pile of ash. Shortly afterwards, the city of Verulanium (modern-day St Albans) suffered the same fate.

The episode was known to contemporaries as 'the fury': an anti-Roman rage that would stop at nothing – that would not shy from the very worst atrocities, even against women and children. To unleash such unflinching terror, something extraordinary must have happened.

And it had.

In the first century AD, as many as 50,000 Roman soldiers were stationed in Britain, almost one-eighth of the total military force of the Empire. This figure alone tells you all you need to know about what a troublesome, rebellion-prone place Britain was: while many tribes sued for peace and numerous native chiefs and aristocrats clearly saw the benefits of becoming Romanised – wine! luxury goods! toilets! – sedition was never far away. Especially as the Romans insisted on acting like every clichéd strutting bad guy you've ever seen in the movies.

When Prasutagus, king of the Iceni, died in AD 60, the Roman civilian and military elite on the ground idiotically chose not to negotiate a new deal with the friendly kingdom, but to treat that kingdom as if it was an enemy. The Icenian royal family was dispossessed and treated like slaves, money and estates were stolen, and nobles were bankrupted and evicted.

At the heart of this was a dynastic problem: Prasutagus had no son, and had left half of his kingdom to be shared between his two young daughters. The Romans feared the instability this would cause, and so decided to make a pre-emptive hostile takeover of the Icenian assets. A group of Roman soldiers raped the two girls – an extraordinary event inasmuch as rape, far from being condoned, was subject to severe punishment in the Roman army. The legal writer Ruffus stated that 'a soldier who takes a girl by force and rapes her shall have his nose cut off, and the girl be given a third part of his property'. Also extraordinary was the public flogging of Prasutagus' widow – for free women could not be legally flogged. And the queen was definitely a free woman.

Her name, by the way, was Boudicca.

It was Boudicca who unleashed the fury that left perhaps 50,000 corpses in the ashes of Camulodunam, Londinium and Verulanium. It was Boudicca who commanded the forces that cut the IX Legion to pieces. And it was the warrior-queen Boudicca who foolishly led a vast and unruly British horde against a fully formed Roman army in a pitched battle somewhere in Warwickshire. Despite a superiority of numbers, the native forces lacked the steely discipline of Roman battlecraft. It was one of the greatest slaughters of all time. The Roman writer Tacitus crowed that 80,000 Britons were killed that day – clearly an exaggeration, but no one knows by how much. The body count almost certainly numbered in the tens of thousands. Boudicca herself was killed or committed suicide.

Paulinus, the Roman general who defeated Boudicca, was another type we all recognise: the 'take no prisoners' career soldier for whom the only option is to always escalate the violence. Having destroyed the main rebel force, Paulinus cut and burned a reign of terror across southern England. Not surprisingly, this just provoked more resistance, and it took another year (and reinforcements from the Continent) before the rebellion was finally contained. At one point, the Empire had even contemplated abandoning Britain altogether. The Boudiccan revolt was a brief candle, and a failure. But it had put the lie to the invincibility of Rome.

ANOTHER BRICK IN THE WALL

'The Roman Conquest was, however, a Good Thing,
since the Britons were only natives at that time.'

Sellar and Yeatman, *1066 and All That*, 1930

The Roman army reached lowland Scotland in AD 79. Their objective was to secure the fertile cornfields of Fife and the Lothians, and to this end they built the Gask Ridge, the first artificial frontier in the Empire. A line of forts and watchtowers running diagonally north-east through Stirlingshire, Perthshire and Angus, it looked out towards the Highlands, an area difficult to police and with no obvious resources. In 83 a huge Roman army marched into Aberdeenshire and, at an unidentified location known as Mons Graupius, utterly smashed a confederation of Caledonian tribes. By 86, however, trouble elsewhere in the Empire led to the withdrawal of legions and the abandonment of the Gask Ridge. 'Britain was completely conquered,' wrote the Roman historian Tacitus in disgust, 'and straight away let go.'

In 122 the Emperor Hadrian, at the head of a huge fleet, arrived on the River Tyne. The early second century was a period of consolidation within the Roman Empire: conquest for its own sake was becoming too expensive. A frontier had already been established to mark the northern limits of imperial writ in Germany; now it was time for north Britannia to be similarly demarcated. This frontier, however, was to be no mere wooden palisade that would rot in

Milecastle 39 of Hadrian's Wall.

the endless rain and have to be replaced regularly. No, this was to be something new: a massive wall built of stone, a defended fortification that stretched from sea to sea on the neck of land between present-day Carlisle and Newcastle. There had been nothing like it in Britain before, and there would be nothing even approaching its scale and ambition for at least another 1,000 years. The logistics were immense, especially as this was still – particularly in the centre and west – hostile territory. The land wall is 73 miles long and is flanked along the west coast by a sea wall of at least 26 miles in length. A deep and wide defensive ditch runs along the northern side and garrisoned forts dot the entire length. It took just three years to build and, despite the wear and tear of centuries, much of it is still in glowering form today.

The wall quickly entered British mythology, and looking at it today you can see why: to cultures where the apex of architecture was a circular hut of thatch and wattle, this colossal stone construction might as well have been emblazoned with a slogan (in Latin, of course): Don't Even Think About It.

Not that the wall was itself much of a fighting platform. The wall-walk was too narrow to defend easily, and (unlike in medieval castles) you couldn't fire obliquely along the outside length from most positions. No, what it was most of all was a barrier. It divided dangerous tribes one from the other, and prevented bands of hostile warriors from moving south easily. It also disrupted the activities of sheep- and cattle-rustlers, and meant that life on the southern side of the wall was generally less troubled than the wild lands to the north. And, of course, the wall served to support the overriding Roman activity: making money. The gates of the wall were usually open, so that traders and others could pass through – and pay passage tax.

Hadrian died in 138. By 140 the legions, in a change of policy, were again pushing north into southern Scotland, operating with their usual ruthlessness: at the fort of Newstead, on the River Tweed, the heads of enemy warriors were spitted on poles and set up at the gates. Another wall – this one of turf – was constructed between the Forth and the Clyde. Hadrian's Wall was still fit for purpose, but Hadrian was now repudiated by the current emperor, Antoninus, and the stone wall was all but deserted, the gates being removed and the garrisons scaled back to a skeleton crew. After just fifteen years, however, the Antonine Wall was abandoned and Hadrian's Wall was back in fashion again: such are the whims of emperors and empires.

In the 180s, chaos in the Empire prompted a native attack on the eastern part of Hadrian's Wall, with Roman soldiers massacred. It took at least two years for the legions to restore order, and the whole of southern Scotland was entirely abandoned. For the warlords and bards of the Celtic tribes, this must have seemed like a great victory. In 208, however, the Emperor Severus was back in the Scottish lowlands with an enormous army and fleet. No pitched battles took place, but new forts were built and the de facto frontier was now set at the River Tay. There were periods of brief conflict followed by longer periods of peace.

But then came the Barbarian Conspiracy.

INVASION! (BARBARIAN STYLE)

'Swords glinted all around and the flames crackled.'

Gildas, The Ruin and Conquest of Britain, *around 540*

By the fourth century, the greatest empire the world had ever seen was on the ropes – and everyone knew it, including the 'barbarian' peoples looking in from the outside of the *Pax Romanica* (Roman Peace). In 367, several different peoples combined in a co-ordinated attack on the province of Britannia. This Barbarian Conspiracy saw the Picts from northern Scotland burst through Hadrian's Wall on the east, while a tribe called the Atecotti (who may have been from the Hebrides or western Scotland) attacked on the west. Across the Irish Sea came a tribe from Ireland known as the Scots (of whom more later). Germanic groups, the Franks and the Saxons, meanwhile raided Gaul and the south of England. For two years the province descended into utter chaos, a catastrophe of murder, rape and pillage far worse than that inflicted by Boudicca's forces. It wasn't until 369 that an effective military response by Rome hunted down the roaming war bands and again secured peace.

Then, in 402, cash to pay the army and imperial administration stopped arriving in the province. In 408, a coalition of Romano-British aristocrats and Roman soldiers announced a virtual unilateral declaration of independence: no one in Rome really noticed, and two years later the beleaguered Empire had washed its hands of its rainy northern colony altogether.

You've seen all those post-apocalyptic movies, where small bands of humans are forced to survive in conditions that only a few years earlier would have been unthinkably primitive. The archaeological record suggests that for the 'civilised' Romano-British of the towns and villas, that apocalypse was on its way. After 430, coinage ceased to circulate, and mass-produced pottery was no longer made. Grass and trees grew along Hadrian's Wall, and in the towns, water and sewage systems broke down. Abandoned villas became squatters' paradises. Fields turned to thorn. A welter of Celtic kinglets and warlords grew up, many of them from families that only a few years before had been sporting the toga. In this post-Roman wilderness, we catch a glimpse of a war leader called Arthur, possibly operating in southern Scotland, but nothing certain can be said about this supposed Arthur of the Britons.

We do know that from around the year 428 waves of invaders, often arriving in small groups at different parts of the coast, were changing Britain forever. Some were hired mercenaries, some were colonists looking for a piece of decent farmland, and some were opportunist thugs intent on piracy and plunder. The decline of Roman power had set off a series of migrations which, perhaps under population pressure, climate change or to escape from enemies, saw different peoples set out for new homes. A number of Germanic peoples, including the Angles, Saxons and Jutes, landed their ships along the east and south coasts. The Jutes, who supposedly colonised Kent, Dorset and the Isle of Wight, have largely disappeared from written history, while their cousins came later to be known as the Anglo-Saxons, giving name to such areas as East Anglia (land of the East Angles) and Wessex (kingdom of the West Saxons).

Slowly, slowly, power was transferred piecemeal from the Celtic-speaking Britons (some of whom still used Latin for their inscriptions) to the Germanic-speaking newcomers. Sometimes this would be at the point of a sword, while political alliances, dynastic marriages and blatant bribery would also have played their part. The Celtic kingdom of Elmet, centred on Leeds, lasted until 617. Cumbria was still speaking British (also known as Old Welsh) three centuries later. The newcomers did not push into Wales, which largely remained British/Celtic, and Cornwall was a British kingdom until its defeat in 838. By this date it is possible to think of the Anglo-Saxons as something new: the English. Meanwhile, the Scots from Ireland established colonies on the west coast of Pictland in the 500s; by the mid-ninth century the Picts had been culturally eclipsed, and eventually northern Britain became known as the land of the Scots. And so, in the Dark Ages we finally see the emergence of national and cultural identities that we recognise, however dimly, through the centuries: English, Scottish and Welsh. Ireland, having never been invaded by Rome, retained much of its traditional Iron Age culture, including Druids and paganism, until the later incursions of Christianity.

During the Dark Ages, fire and sword were undoubtedly much in evidence, although the records are scant (which itself reveals a great deal about the decay of learning and administration). But there was probably something else as well. The population of Roman Britain was at least 4 million, if not more, while the Domesday Book survey of 1086 suggests an English population of less than 3 million – and that was after several generations of growth. What had happened to the missing millions? A hint may be found in the *Anglo-Saxon Chronicle* and the Venerable Bede's *The Ecclesiastical History of the English People*, both of which mention 'a great pestilence' in the seventh century. Perhaps an epidemic had ravaged the country, to be followed by the inevitable famine.

Blood, fire, plague, institutional collapse and no decent toilets for the next 1,000 years: welcome to the Dark Ages.

MAY THE FORCE BE WITH YOU

*'Never until now in this island, as books and scholars of old inform us,
was there greater slaughter of an army with the sword's edge.'*

Anglo-Saxon Chronicle

This is a family saga: a story of a father, son, and grandson. The father is one of the most famous figures in Dark Age history, but his equally capable descendents are almost unknown – which is strange, considering the grandson was the first man to be regarded by his contemporaries as a king of all England.

England in the ninth and tenth centuries was a patchwork of regional Anglo-Saxon kingships whose power and territory waxed and waned depending on the strength of their respective war-kings and relationships with their neighbours. To make a complex story simple, Northumbria ('north of the Humber') held most of the north, with Mercia in the Midlands, East Anglia to the east and, in the south and south-west, Wessex.

And then came the Vikings.

The Vikings knew a good thing when they saw one. Ever since their first raid on England – in 793, in which they bespattered the undefended monastery at Lindisfarne with the blood of monks – they had cultivated a fearsome reputation. After a while they didn't even need to bother with the smash-and-grab raids – the terrified or defeated Anglo-Saxon communities were willing to buy them off with silver, gold or horses. Soon, wholesale extortion became the name of the Viking game. From 865, however, the Viking strategy changed again: to occupation. From now on they were bent on conquest. East Anglia as an independent kingdom ceased to exist; Mercia tottered; a puppet ruler was set up in Northumbria; it was obvious that Wessex was next.

An over-elaborate nineteenth-century view of Alfred the Great.

By 871, the royal family of Wessex had lost four successive leaders, all sons of King Aethulwulf, who had died in 858. The fifth and final son, Alfred, was in his early 20s, and had already spent five years facing the foe. The fight against the Vikings defined his entire life, and in later centuries his name gained the ultimate accolade of popular history: he became Alfred the Great.

The *Anglo-Saxon Chronicle*, our best record of these turbulent centuries, uses many terms for the Vikings, but the mobile army ravaging the country in pursuit of conquest was normally grouped under one name: the Force. In the first seven years of Alfred's reign, the war swung back and forth. After one defeat, he paid off the Vikings – the usual practice – and the Force moved on to take over Mercia, leaving Wessex as the last independent kingdom in England. Then came breathing space, when 120 Viking ships were destroyed in a great storm, with the loss of perhaps 3,600 warriors. Not for the last time, the English Channel proved to be the ultimate bulwark against invaders. In 878, however, the Vikings were back, and Wessex was almost entirely conquered. Alfred hid out in the Somerset marshes, at his lowest ebb. The story of the burning of the cakes is probably a later invention – but, apparently through sheer force of will and a bucketload of charisma, Alfred rallied his troops and five months later they defeated the Force in open combat at the Battle of Edington ('There he fought with the whole Force and put them to flight', says the *Chronicle*). This was followed by a siege of the Viking fort at Chippenham, which resulted in total victory for the men of Wessex. The war dragged on piecemeal for years, but Alfred had preserved his independence.

The Viking-dominated eastern half of England, from the Thames to the Tees, was known as the Danelaw. Alfred's son Edward the Elder – whom hardly anyone has heard of – equalled if not surpassed his father's achievements by conquering the Danelaw as far as the River Humber, and absorbing Mercia and East Anglia into his own kingdom.

And then we come to the next undeserved unknown, Athelstan, Edward's son, and king from 924. Athelstan pushed even further north, bringing Northumbria to heel. Wessex was now in effect the regional superpower, and its neighbours' traditional enmities and conflicts were forgotten in the light of this expansive, aggressive common enemy. In 937, Athelstan faced a combined army consisting of a triple alliance: the men of Olaf Guthfrithsson, the Viking King of Dublin; the army of Constantine II, King of Scots; and the forces of the Welsh-speaking Britons of Strathclyde (modern-day north-west England and south-west Scotland).

The *Anglo-Saxon Chronicle* is often terse, even brusque, in its description of events. For the great Battle of Brunanburh, however, it becomes positively poetic: 'Athelstan ... broke the shield-wall, hewed linden-wood with hammers leaving ... The field was slick with men's blood ... many a man lay wrecked by spears, northern warrior shot over shield ... West-Saxons went forth all the day long on

EDWARD the ELDER

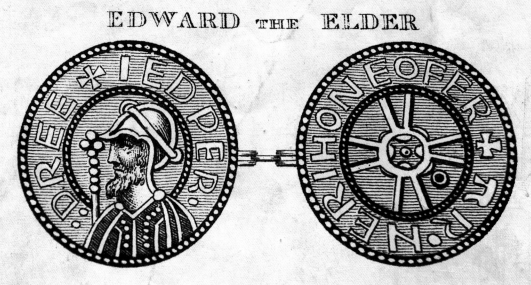

Edward the Elder, as pictured on one of his coins.

the enemy's tracks, hewing the fleeing forces from behind with blades new-sharpened.' The aftermath is grimly rendered: 'They left behind them sharing the dead the dusk-dressed one, the black raven, with hard beak of horn, and hoary-coated eagle, white-tailed, eating the carrion, greedy war-hawk, and that grey beast, the wolf of the wood.' Sadly the site of Brunanburh has never been identified, so we cannot walk the battlefield with a guide intoning these powerful lines in suitably Gothic fashion.

The crushing victory at Brunanburh affirmed Athelstan as the greatest Anglo-Saxon leader of his age. It also confirmed him as something entirely new: the king, not just of Wessex, land of the West-Saxons, but of all England. The Force was with him.

THE ST BRICE'S DAY MASSACRE

'All the Danes ... to be destroyed by a most just extermination.'

King Aethelred the Unraed, 1002

The Vikings did not go away. Although many were now farmers and landowners in the east and north-east of England – the Danelaw, where civil matters were often resolved using the Scandinavian legal code – others were freebooters, pirates and mercenaries, the latter available for hire to solve local disputes with axe and sword. And they often didn't go home afterwards. In the late tenth century, it was common for many towns in southern England to have 'a Viking problem' – a small group of hard-drinking, hard-living Dark Age Hell's Angels making a nuisance of themselves by leeching off the local community. They probably had their own equivalent of a bikers' bar.

In 980, serious raiding commenced again. Between 991 and 994, the Anglo-Saxon King Aethelred the Unraed (often translated as 'the unready' but more accurately as 'the ill-advised' or 'ill-counselled') paid 26,000 pounds in silver as protection money. But the bad guys kept coming. Another 24,000 pounds of silver was handed over early in 1002. The Vikings were bleeding England dry.

Then, in 1002, Aethelred made an alliance with the powerful Duke of Normandy. Newly emboldened, he decided to wipe out the brutish thugs who were making his kingdom's life a misery. On St Brice's Day, 13 November, he issued a nation-wide order: 'That all the Danes who had sprung up in this island, sprouting like cockle [weeds] amongst the wheat, were to be destroyed by a most just extermination, and this decree was to be put into effect even as far as death.'

Massacre of the Danes on St Brice's Day.

No one knows how many Danes were murdered that day. Almost certainly no executions were carried out in the Danelaw, where the numbers would have been far too great to overcome – and anyway, many 'Danes' in the Danelaw were increasingly thinking of themselves as English. More likely, the black ops killings occurred in places where bands of Vikings had established themselves as unwelcome visitors – places like Oxford.

In 2008, a mass grave was uncovered during building work at an Oxford college. Between thirty-four and thirty-eight men, all taller than the average Anglo-Saxon, and powerfully built, had been killed and dumped in a ditch outside the city limits. Twenty-seven had been clubbed to death. Twelve had been stabbed in the back. One had been decapitated. Many had suffered burns. A number were related to each other.

Remarkably, the bodies could be traced to an actual historical event, one recorded by Aethelred himself in a charter to the Oxford church of St Fridewide:

... those Danes who dwelt [in Oxford], striving to escape death, entered this sanctuary of Christ, having broken by force the doors and bolts, and resolved to make a refuge and defence for themselves therein against the people of the town and suburbs; but when all the people in pursuit strove, forced by necessity, to drive them out, and could not, they set fire to the planks and burnt, as it seems, this church with its ornaments and books.

Another example of the national St Brice's Massacre was uncovered in 2009, near Weymouth in Dorset. Here, the mass grave revealed the skeletons of fifty-four strongly built Viking warriors, all of whom had been decapitated with swords and dumped in an abandoned quarry.

One of those murdered on that fateful November day was Gunnhild, the sister of King Svein Forkbeard of Denmark. She was beheaded along with her husband, Pallig Tokesen, a Viking mercenary who himself had taken part in raids on the very England where he had settled. The following year Svein fell upon the English like the wolf upon the fold, his killing frenzy probably in part motivated by revenge. After more than a decade of vicious fighting, Anglo-Saxon England fell to the Viking yoke. In 1017 Cnut, Svein's son, was crowned King of England. The St Brice's Day Massacre had turned out be a very bad piece of advice indeed.

St John's College, Oxford,
where the mass grave was found.
(LOC, LC-DIG-ppmsc-08772)

AD 1066

LAST STAND AT STAMFORD BRIDGE

'Heroes must write their histories in the blood of many corpses.'

Peter Brent, The Viking Saga, 1975

The Viking army was virtually off-duty as it marched through the bright September morning in the East Riding of Yorkshire. Five days earlier it had defeated a formidable English force at the Battle of Fulford, and York had fallen without a murmur. The people of the North had agreed to join them on a southward march which would no doubt see a Norwegian on the throne of England. The English king, Harold I, was far to the south, looking across the Channel for an expected invasion from Normandy. There was no immediate threat in Yorkshire and, the day being unseasonably warm, many of the Vikings had left their chainmail shirts back at their ships.

Then something strange glittered on the horizon. As the Norsemen came closer to the crossing of the River Derwent at the place later known as Stamford Bridge, they realised that they were looking at a vast horde of armed men: King Harold had done the impossible, force-marching his army 200 miles from the south coast in just six days.

Three riders were immediately despatched to the anchored Viking ships 12 miles away, to bring reinforcements and the much-needed chainmail. But the English, having spent the summer at arms waiting for an invasion that was always promised but never materialised, were in no mood to wait. The Norsemen who had already crossed the river were wiped out – then a lone Viking, his eyes wild with berserker rage, stepped onto the planking of the narrow bridge. Berserkers were justly feared as Viking killing machines, their physiology so amplified that they were impervious to all but the most serious of wounds. One by one, individual Anglo-Saxons charged along the bottleneck, and one by one their hacked and slashed bodies ended up in the Derwent. According to the legend, as many as forty men perished this way before one canny warrior waded into midstream below the bridge and thrust a spear up through a gap in the timbers and into the berserker's testicles.

On the east bank, standing beside his 'Landwaster' standard, stood Harald Hardrada, King of Norway and a man sometimes called 'the Last Viking'. Immensely tall and strong, his military career had seen him work as a mercenary in Russia,

28

Constantinople and Sicily. He had fought against Muslim armies and Christian foes, and had been a member of the elite Byzantine imperial guard (he had also pulled out the eyes of one deposed emperor). His was a life dedicated entirely to fighting and plundering (even as his invasion fleet had approached England, he couldn't resist expending a little excess energy on devastating some ill-defended coastal settlements in the north-east; once a Viking, always a Viking). Now, with the bridge open and the enemy hordes pouring across, it was time to die in a manner as befitted a hero of the sagas.

Hardrada was in his 50s, but age had not dimmed his prowess. As the English pressed forward, he gripped his great sword with both hands and cleaved flesh and bone with a terrifying intensity until he was brought to his knees by an arrow to the windpipe. As he collapsed, his lungs filling with blood, his last-stand guards were cut down to a man.

At this point, the Viking reinforcements arrived, exhausted by their 12-mile run in full chainmail. The English too were almost at the end of their strength, and for a time it looked as if the Norsemen

would triumph, but eventually their lines broke under a last desperate English charge, and the scattered survivors were picked off as they fled towards their ships. Among the dead was Tostig, the brother of the English king Harold, who had treacherously allied with Hardrada after having been driven out from his earldom of Northumbria.

Hardrada's invasion fleet, combined with Tostig's forces and Northmen recruited from Orkney, had numbered some 300 ships. Only twenty-four were required to bring the survivors home.

After an interval of Viking rule under Cnut and his sons, the throne of England had returned to the House of Wessex in 1042. The country, however, was only to remain Anglo-Saxon for another twenty-four years. The battle of Stamford Bridge was fought on Monday, 25 September 1066. On the following Wednesday, the long-awaited change in the wind finally allowed Duke William of Normandy to sail his invasion fleet across the English Channel. In the middle of the night William's flagship suddenly found itself alone in open waters, the slower transports nowhere in sight. Had the English warships appeared at this point, the Norman Conquest would have been over before it began. As it was, William quietly rode at anchor until the rest of his fleet appeared, and at daylight the Normans landed unopposed at Pevensey Bay.

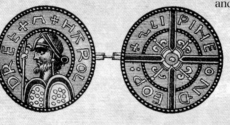

A coin and portrait of Harold I.

King Harold was at York when he heard the news. Thirteen days later he was near the south coast, and on 14 October he was dead, cut to pieces by William's knights at the Battle of Hastings. Hardrada had been no pushover, and Harold's army had been severely mauled in the conflict. In addition, the forces of Harold's loyal earls Edwin and Morcar had been so depleted at the defeat of Fulford that they could not muster assistance for Harold against William. That, combined with the exhaustion brought on by two amazingly fast forced marches up and down the length of England, meant that the English army at Hastings was not at anywhere near its full strength or capability. The year 1066 started with England ruled by an Anglo-Saxon king (Harold was crowned on 6 January, one day after the death of Edward the Confessor). In September it looked as if there would be a Norwegian on the throne; and by October the three-way contest had been decided in favour of an illegitimate Norman Duke whose ancestors had once been Vikings.

Once upon a time, the people of Stamford Bridge regularly commemorated the battle by baking 'spear pies', boat-shaped pies fitted with a skewer shaped like the weapon that unmanned the Viking berserker. Sadly this tradition seems to have last been enacted in 1966, on the 900th anniversary of a battle that, through its ultimate effects, changed England forever.

AD 1069

THE HARRYING OF THE NORTH

'I became a barbarous murderer of many thousands.'

William the Conqueror

100,000. That's the guesstimate for the number of people killed in Britain's largest ever act of genocide (in fact the true figure may be even higher – perhaps as much as 150,000). Strangely enough, many history books make only a glancing reference to this slaughter, if they mention it at all. Possibly because it did not take place in the south of England, but 'oop north', in what has been seen as the far less 'important' upland region beyond the River Humber.

Welcome to the north-south divide, eleventh-century style.

The instigator of the massacre was William the Conqueror, known variously as Duke Guillaume of Normandy, King William I of England, and – on account of his illegitimacy – William the Bastard. Bill the Bastard, as he was never called, is, of course, most famous for his victory at the Battle of Hastings in 1066, which saw the death of King Harold I and the subsequent extinction of the Anglo-Saxon royal family. After Hastings, William let his army loose for a bit of rape and pillage in parts of Kent, and then, before entering the capital, went on a semi-circular tour of the outskirts of London, devastating the

land so dreadfully that it took a generation for some villages to recover. Only then did he have himself crowned king. All this set the tone for the Norman Conquest: a regime change that was as efficient and organised as it was pitiless and brutal.

William, however, did not have it all his own way. In the years after 1066, a rash of short-lived rebellions broke out in Wales, the west, the south-west, the east, the Midlands and the North. In 1069, the North rose again. William had had to deal with two revolts in Yorkshire and Northumbria already, and in each case he had thought the area 'pacified'. But each time, the warrior bands had simply melted into the hills, and the punishments William inflicted on the area, although severe, had not removed the military threat posed by the men of the North.

By the winter of 1069 William had had enough. His new strategy was simple: just kill everyone.

The rebel warriors depended on the peasants to farm the land and bring in the harvest. If there were no peasants, there would be no farming and no food. William's army swept through a large swathe of north-east England, burning every village and killing every man, woman, child, cow, ox and horse they could find. Stores of grain and seeds were destroyed. Barns put to the torch. Farming implements broken up and smashed. Soldiers killed more people than they could remember. The roads and fields stank with the putrefying corpses of humans and animals. Disease broke out. When the spring of 1070 came around, no crops were planted – because there was no one to plant them. An artificial famine was created. Those who did not die of the sword, infection or cold survived by eating dogs and cats or selling themselves into slavery simply in the hope of avoiding starvation. The *Anglo-Saxon Chronicle* recorded the events in its usual clipped style: 'And King William marched into the shire and devastated it completely.'

In 1086, Domesday Book, William's extraordinary economic survey of England, showed that when the monks writing the *Anglo-Saxon Chronicle* used words such as 'devastated' and 'completely', they were not employing such terms lightly. For village after village, Domesday records simply use one term: 'it is waste.' Sixteen years after what became known as the Harrowing (or Harrying) of the North, the population had not returned. What were once fertile fields and productive farms were still nettle and weed. The land was empty. A Durham writer said that not a single person could be found in the villages between York and Durham. Such were the consequences of genocide.

William was no armchair general. After the annihilation of the north he was faced with another revolt, this one in North Wales, and he personally led his troops in a hazardous winter march over the Pennines, his fortitude and perseverance inspiring his men to keep going in appalling conditions. In 1071, William finally defeated Hereward the Wake, whose guerrilla bands had fought an effective resistance campaign from the fens of East Anglia, and the following year William launched a great expedition by sea and land into Scotland – the Scots having supported the anti-Norman rebellions in the North of England – and humbled King Malcolm at Abernethy in Perthshire. Over the next fifteen years William was almost continuously at war, in either England or Normandy. His campaigns were characterised by their combination of brutality and rapidity – he might be said to have invented the concept of blitzkrieg.

William died in 1087, in France. According to the Anglo-Norman chronicler Ordericus Vitalis, the king made a deathbed confession regretting the Harrying of the North:

> I have persecuted the natives of England beyond all reason. Whether gentle or simple I have cruelly oppressed them; many I unjustly disinherited; innumerable multitudes perished through me by famine or the sword ... I fell on the English of the northern shires like a ravening lion. I commanded their houses and corn, with all their implements and chattels, to be burnt without distinction, and great herds of cattle and beasts of burden to be butchered whenever they are found. In this way I took revenge on multitudes of both sexes by subjecting them to the calamity of a cruel famine, and so became a barbarous murderer of many thousands, both young and old, of that fine race of people.

Ordericus was not present at the scene (being only 12 years old at the time) and was writing many years after the fact, so you may have your own opinions about the reliability of his account. Nevertheless, there is a chilling grace to Ordericus' words, a suitable endnote for the ruthless man they called the Conqueror: 'innumerable multitudes perished through me by famine or the sword ...'

Durham Castle and cathedral, built after the conquest of the region as a sign of Norman power. Not one living person, it was said, could be found in the villages between here and York. (LOC, LC-DIG-ppmsc-08358)

ANARCHY IN THE UK

'Destroy!'

The Sex Pistols, 'Anarchy in the UK', 1977

Everyday life down at the abbey during the Anarchy.

Let us make the acquaintance of Geoffrey de Mandeville, Earl of Essex and robber baron of the highest magnitude. After a life of violence, the 'terrible earl', as he came to be called, retired to the fens of East Anglia, kicked out the monks from Ramsey Abbey, fortified the town of Ely and proceeded to launch a campaign of fire and blood on Cambridge and the surrounding area so devastating that neither ox nor plough could be seen for a space of 30 miles. Torture, murder, rape, church-burning and enslavement became par for the course.

De Mandeville's excesses were made possible because England was in the grip of a vicious civil war known as the Anarchy. Two claimants for the throne – Matilda, the daughter of Henry I, and Stephen, Henry's nephew – were slogging it out across Middle England in an endless series of raids, skirmishes, and sieges, with Worcestershire, Gloucestershire, Oxfordshire, Wiltshire and Dorset at the heart of the killing fields. With central authority in meltdown, the barons were living up to the highest principles of their class – by stealing everything that wasn't nailed down, and slaughtering anyone who got in the way. Across the country, earls built private castles, raised private armies, invaded estates, and engaged in blood feuds with their neighbours. The highest in the land became exemplars of a new kind of manifest destiny – abjure every oath, break every law, trample on the weak, and inflict the worst kind of cruelties, all so as long as you end up with more land and money than your rivals.

In an eyewitness account, the monk who wrote *The Peterborough Chronicle* described the Anarchy in vivid detail:

> Every chieftain made castles and held them against the king; and they filled the land full of castles. They viciously oppressed the poor men of the land with castle-building work; when the castles were made, then they filled the land with devils and evil men. Then they seized those who had any goods, both by night and day, working men and women, and threw them into prison and tortured them for gold and silver with uncountable tortures, for never was there a martyr so tortured as these men were ... One they hung by his feet and filled his lungs with smoke. One was hung up by the thumbs and another by the head and had coats of mail hung on his feet. One they put a knotted cord about his head and twisted it so that it went into the brains ...

King's College in Cambridge, founded by Henry VI. However, in this era the king looked rather less kindly upon the city, and sacked it without mercy. (LOC, LC-DIG-ppmsc-08084)

After more revolting descriptions of the tortures employed in the barons' dungeons, the chronicler continued: 'Many thousands they wore out with hunger. I neither can nor may recount all the atrocities nor all the tortures that they did on wretched men in this land ... they spared neither church nor churchyard, but took all the goods that were therein, and then burned the church ... and every man robbed another who could.' The account finished with heart-rending poetic imagery: 'To till the ground was to plough the sea: the earth bare no corn, for the land was all laid waste by such deeds; and they said openly, that Christ slept, and his saints.'

Southgate Street, Gloucester. The city was a stronghold for Matilda. (LOC, LC-DIG-ppmsc-08406)

Stephen seems not to have been very wise, but he was well-liked by those around him, and he was a formidable warrior with an apparently genuine dedication to the ideals of chivalry – always preferring the 'fair fight' to a winning but dishonourably superior position. In 1141, six years after he had been crowned the actual king, he was engaged by Earl Rannulf's forces at Lincoln, where he is described as fighting 'like a lion at bay', taking on all comers with his sword until it snapped, and then laying about him with a Danish axe until that too shattered. Felled by a stone, he finally surrendered to the Earl of Gloucester – Matilda's brother. With Stephen in chains in Bristol, Matilda was declared queen but never crowned, her eight-month reign a catalogue of disasters stemming largely from her own arrogant personality. Expelled from London, Matilda's forces retreated through Oxford and Winchester – much of the latter being burned to the ground – and took refuge in their West Country powerbase at Gloucester. The Earl of Gloucester, however, was captured, and was only set at liberty in exchange for the release of Stephen.

King Stephen being captured.

The year 1141 was the height of the Anarchy, but the wearisome fighting continued for another seven long years before Matilda finally acknowledged hers was a lost cause and departed for northern France. Even then, the barons, by now utterly steeped in habitual violence, continued to despoil the country until 1153.

Geoffrey de Mandeville, meanwhile, defied every attempt by Stephen to dislodge him from his fenland fastness. Then in August 1144, while attacking Stephen's unfinished castle at Burwell in Cambridgeshire, he was struck by a chance arrow. The wound was mortal. It couldn't have happened to a nicer fellow.

THE JEWISH MASSACRE AT YORK

'Many people in the county of York ... without any scruple of Christian conscientiousness, thirsted for their perfidious blood, through the desire of plunder.'

William of Newburgh, History of English Affairs, *twelfth century*

Inside the castle, the food and water had been exhausted. Outside, a screaming mob had besieged the walls for six days, howling for blood. Faced with the inevitable, the men of York's Jewish community took the hardest decisions of their lives: they killed their wives and children, and then knelt as the rabbi took his knife and cut their throats one by one. The few who chose to avoid suicide opened the gates and swore they would convert to Christianity if their lives were spared: they were slaughtered to the last man.

The massacre of the Jews of York on 16 March 1190 saw the deaths of 150 men, women and children – the town's entire Jewish community. It was, in a way, collateral damage from the greatest military adventure of the day: the Crusades.

The Jews had arrived in England after the Norman Conquest of 1066, specifically invited for their financial role; by 1190 there were probably 2,500 in the country. Moneylending, or usury, was forbidden to Christians – but not to Jews. Merchants, abbots, nobles and kings alike flocked to the 'Jewish banks' to finance their enterprises, abbey- or castle-building, and wars. In return, the Jews charged interest on the loans – and hence a number became very rich. Aaron of Lincoln, for example, who died in 1186, was probably the wealthiest man in Norman England, his personal fortune outstripping that of the king. The Jews' financial success, combined with their visible 'difference' expressed through clothing and hairstyles, soon brought forth not just resentment, but outright hatred. To this was added the 'blood libel', a ludicrous but nonetheless widespread belief that Jews kidnapped and murdered Christian children for their own religious rituals.

In 1189 the Third Crusade was launched. Shortly after his coronation, Richard the Lionheart declared he would liberate the ancient Christian sites of the Holy Land from Muslim occupying forces, and the entire country became giddy with Crusade fever. Popular emotion found a convenient target in the 'enemy within': thirty Jews were killed in London, and fifty-seven in Bury St Edmunds.

Further riots broke out in Norwich, King's Lynn, Stamford and Lincoln. Then it was the turn of York to feel the anti-Semitic wrath. Six months earlier, the wealthy Benedict of York had been badly wounded during the pogrom in London. He tried to return home but died in Northampton, having been subjected to a forced conversion to Christianity. In March 1190, the York mob burned Benedict's house and murdered his widow and children. Other homes were set ablaze and plundered. The rest of the Jewish community hid in York's wooden castle. As the chronicler William of Newburgh wrote, 'the zeal of the Christian people was roused, and immense bands of armed men, not only from the city, but also from the county, gathered around the castle'. Siege engines were brought to bear against the castle's walls. After six days, the place of refuge became a tomb.

The besiegers included several monks and priests, who spouted incessant anti-Jewish venom. In addition, there were many men about to leave on Crusade who were clearly aware that, once having departed the shores of England, they were hardly likely to be tracked down and punished for anything they might do in York that day. Others expressed the view that any sins they committed would be washed away by the 'good deeds' they were to perform on their 'holy war' (as we know now, of course, the Crusades were little more than badly organised, badly led bouts of slaughter-by-numbers – nothing 'holy' about them at all).

The real key to the grim events at York, however, can be found in what happened next. The mob stormed the minster and burned all the bonds of debts to Jews that were kept there. At a stroke, the barons, landowners and merchants who had borrowed money from the Jews were debt-free. Part of the mob's fury was indeed simple Jew-hating; but a significant number of the higher-class participants (including a debt-ridden noble named Richard Malebisse) had good financial reasons to see the Jews dead and their financial records burned. The complete annihilation of the Jewish community in York was accomplished by a volatile and murderous mixture of religious prejudice and sordid self-interest.

Following the calamitous events of 1189–90, the Jews of England continued to live in an uneasy peace. In 1279, some 300 Jews were executed on suspicion of counterfeiting and clipping coins (cutting the valuable metal off the edge of coins). Eleven years later, King Edward I passed the Edict of Expulsion of 1290, which saw all Jews banished from the kingdom. Jews did not return to England until the 'Resettlement' of 1655.

At York, a plaque stands at the spot of the massacre, which is now occupied by the later stone-built Clifford Tower. The memorial reads: 'On the night of Friday 16 March 1190 some 150 Jews and Jewesses of York having sought protection in the Royal Castle on this site from a mob incited by Richard Malebisse and others chose to die at each other's hands rather than renounce their faith.'

AD 1192

RICHARD AND JOHN: BROTHERS IN ARMS

'I am become as it were a monster unto many.'

Psalm lxxi, 6

In the Middle Ages, legitimate male heirs were more important than gold – the common saying was that families needed at least 'an heir and a spare'. Long-lived Henry II, King of England from 1154, had an astonishing superabundance of sons who reached adulthood – four in total. Henry, the eldest, died of dysentery in 1183, however, aged 27. The second son, Geoffrey, perished in a tournament three years later, trampled to death by a horse. This moved the third and fourth sons, Richard and John, up the list. Father and sons also shared a family propensity for extraordinarily choleric temper tantrums, which amazed and terrified all those who witnessed the madness-like episodes. The House of Angevin – their origin was in Anjou in northern France – were reputed to be descended from Melusine, a female demon; Gerald of Wales quotes the family joking about their ancestry: 'Do not deprive us of our heritage; we cannot help acting like devils.' Apparently it was their demonic genes that made them do it.

Richard became king on the death of Henry in 1189, and the following year departed for the Third Crusade. French-born and bred, Richard could not speak English and spent barely twelve months of his nine-and-a-half-year reign in England. The country had its uses, however – it gave him a crown, for a start, and its able tax administration was very handy at squeezing revenues out of all and sundry. Richard was a lover of war above all else. 'He cared,' wrote Gerald of Wales, 'for no success that was not reached by a path cut by his own sword and stained with the blood of his adversaries.' John was universally reviled for having hanged twenty-eight young boys, taken as hostages from Welsh rebels. But it was Richard who put to death 2,700 hostages at the Siege of Acre in the Holy Land, a war crime of such magnitude that only the habitual excesses of a holy war prevented its condemnation.

In 1192 Richard bid farewell to the fruitless slaughter of the Crusade, only to be captured by his enemy Leopold of Austria and subjected to a sordid auction by the crowned heads of Europe for a share of his ransom. John, having already run a near state-within-a-state in his brother's absence, promptly declared himself King of England, even though it was known that Richard was still alive.

In March 1194 Richard, now ransomed, finally returned to England, and most of the castles that had declared for John swiftly capitulated; the keeper of St Michael's Mount in Cornwall is supposed to have died of fright on hearing the news that the Lionheart was back. Only the Nottingham garrison held out, simply because they refused to believe the king had truly returned to England. Once Richard convinced them in typical fashion – by storming the outer gate of the castle – they too surrendered.

Instead of executing John for treason, Richard humiliated him with kindness, calling his brother 'only a child who has had evil counsellors'. The 'child' was 27 years old at the time. For the next five years he redeemed himself to an extent, proving to be a capable general in the service of Richard's wars in France.

Richard died in 1199, killed at a minor siege in France (at Richard's request, the archer who shot the fatal bolt was indeed spared the noose when the town was captured, but he was flayed alive instead). John was now king, but his reign was not England's finest hour. The rich lands of Normandy were lost; he picked a fight with the Church, which ended with the King of England surrendering his very country to the fealty of the Pope; civil war broke out; and a combined baronial revolt and French invasion saw the loss of London and almost put a French king on the throne. Despite this, John fought a ferocious rearguard action, and was in the slow process of regaining the upper hand when he overindulged in a meal of peaches at Lynn in East Anglia. The jury is out as to whether the surfeit of peaches gave him dysentery or had perhaps been dosed with a slow-acting poison, or whether his illness was entirely unconnected with his fruit binge: whatever the cause, severe abdominal pain swiftly disabled him and, on 18 October 1216, King John died. His 9-year-old son was declared King Henry III and many of the rebels, whose quarrel had been with the father and not the son, made peace. The French invasion faltered and then collapsed when the ships carrying reinforcements were destroyed in the Channel.

St Michael's Mount, whose keeper allegedly died of terror at the Lionheart's return. (LC-DIG-ppmsc-08234)

PIRATES OF THE HIGH SEAS

'No man can live long who spends his days doing ill.'

Anon., Eustace the Monk, *about 1223/1284*

Long before pirates became associated with the Caribbean and saying 'Ha-harr!', men of the sea were attacking and plundering other ships and tipping their unfortunate crews into the sea. Most seagoing nations turned a blind eye to the supposedly universally despised crime of piracy, as long as it was their enemies' vessels that were being robbed or sent to the bottom.

No one in the Middle Ages illustrates this barbarous lifestyle better than the man known to history as Eustace the Monk. The son of a knight from Boulogne, Eustace was educated at a Benedictine monastery and later worked for the Count of Boulogne. However, life as a clerk was not for him – having been outlawed for a number of crimes, he headed a multinational crew of

St Peter's Port, Guernsey, showing Castle Cornet, seized by Eustace the Monk.
(LOC, LC-DIG-ppmsc-08104)

desperadoes who roamed and ruled the Straits of Dover, not caring whose ships they attacked. After a time his services were purchased (expensively) by King John of England, and the 'Black Monk' thereafter concentrated exclusively on French targets.

In 1212, Eustace abandoned John and switched sides to England's enemy, Philip II of France (who had deeper pockets). The English clawed back the Channel Islands, thus depriving Eustace of his permanent base, so the pirate pillaged Folkestone in revenge. But when John died in 1216, the French invasion started running out of friends in England. The following year Eustace was ferrying reinforcements across the Channel when his flotilla encountered a larger force of English ships from the Cinque Ports (Hastings, Romney, Hythe, Dover and Sandwich). Eustace's ships were heavily laden with troops, and impossible to manoeuvre: the English sailed close, to windward, and threw powdered quicklime into the wind. The chemical weapons attack blinded the pirate crew, and they were quickly overcome by a boarding party. Among the prisoners at the Battle of Sandwich were several French nobles, who were worth nice fat ransoms. Eustace, however, found hiding in the bilges, was not so lucky. As the most successful pirate of his age, he was able to offer a vast ransom of £6,600, but it was not accepted. His former #2, Stephen of Winchelsea, dragged Eustace to the ship's rail and decapitated him with a sword. Eustace the Monk then went on a tour of the English coast, where people who had suffered from his depredations came out to spit on his severed head.

Sea warfare, medieval style: archers and boarding parties.

More recently, from the 1550s onward, Falmouth in Cornwall was a pirate haven, where several generations of the powerful Killigrew family operated a criminal syndicate that extended over to Ireland and was effectively a pirating and wrecking mafia, prominent among whom were Lady Killigrew, the matriarch, who fenced pirate loot her entire life, and Elizabeth Killigrew, who personally led an assault on a Spanish merchant vessel sheltering in Falmouth from a storm. In sixteenth-century

Scotland, meanwhile, piracy was almost a way of life for some clans and nobles on the Atlantic seaboard, with Clan MacNeil of Barra in the Outer Hebrides being particular culprits.

By the fourteenth century, monarchs were issuing 'letters of marque' to sea captains. These basically stated that if a merchant had lost money, goods or a ship to say, a French pirate, then the merchant was entitled to attack any other French vessel and take goods to the equivalent value. This was, obviously, just licensed piracy hiding under a legal fiction, something that would be refined in later years by the invention of the 'privateer' – a private vessel given the blessing to attack other ships, as long as they belonged to another country.

In 1569, for example, Englishman and pirate-for-hire Sir Henry Compton was raiding English targets under a privateering licence from France. Five years later the ship he used, the mighty 200-ton *Castle of Comfort*, was under the command of Elizabeth I's privateers and taking French and Spanish vessels (even though England was suppos-edly at peace with both nations – privateering, being war at arm's-length, had the advantage of plausible deniability). In the 1560s, William Hawkins the Younger, the Mayor of Plymouth, was privateering on behalf of one French faction – the Protestants – against the Catholics in that country's religious civil war. For the next two centuries England,

Sea warfare, sixteenth-century style: guns and boarding parties.

Scotland, France, Spain, the Netherlands and the United States of America all used privateers as a way of waging economic warfare on their enemies, even in times of nominal peace. The Black Monk would have been proud.

THE BLOODY FATE OF KINGS

'All Kings is mostly rapscallions.'

Mark Twain, The Adventures of Huckleberry Finn, *1884*

Death attends even the most glorious of kings.

Had insurance companies been operating in the Middle Ages, it would have been well-nigh impossible to take out a policy on a king or a member of the royal family because the chances of an early death – and frequently an unpleasant one – were extraordinarily high. Here we briefly consider the fate of some of these unfortunate individuals.

William II of England (died 1100)

One of the sons of William the Conqueror, William Rufus was a charmless lout who may just as well have had the word T-H-U-G tattooed across his forehead. Out hunting in the New Forest, he found himself the recipient of a fatal crossbow bolt to the chest. All concerned swore that it was simply an accident, but the way the corpse was displayed, and the strange coincidence that William's rival just happened to be loitering a few miles away (close enough to grab the royal treasury at Winchester and instantly proclaim himself king), suggests we are looking at a planned assassination, complete with lone archer and grassy knoll. The beneficiary of this medieval Dealey Plaza was William's younger brother, Henry I.

The Rufus Stone, which marks the spot the king fell.
(LOC, LC-DIG-ppmsc-09012)

Henry I of England (died 1135)

In 1135 Henry was 67 years old – astonishingly ancient for the period – and had been King of England for an equally impressive thirty-five years, surviving an invasion by his brother Robert, wars in France, civil war and numerous battles. After campaigning against rebellious nobles in Normandy, Henry took something of a holiday, with plenty of hunting and feasting. Against his doctor's advice, the old man ate rather too many lampreys – the eel-like fish were regarded as a delicacy in the Middle Ages – and developed an abdominal pain which proved, after much discomfort, terminal. He thus became the only king in history to pass away from a surfeit of lampreys.

Arthur of Brittany (died 1203)

After the Lionheart's death, Arthur, his nephew, 16 years old, found himself John's prisoner. John wanted the boy blinded and castrated, but the man charged with the task refused to carry it out. So one night at Rouen, John, somewhat under the influence of alcohol, murdered Arthur himself (probably by stabbing), roped a heavy stone around the body and threw it into the River Seine. The act not only engendered widespread distaste for John, but it also deprived English history of a real King Arthur.

Edward II of England (died 1327)

After a bitter civil war, Edward was deposed by his wife Isabella and her lover, the powerful Marcher Lord Roger de Mortimer. Imprisoned in Berkeley Castle in Gloucestershire, Edward was pinned to the floor by a door while a horn was pushed into his anus and a red-hot poker thrust into his bowels. He died in agony – and in a manner that made a clear reference to his homosexuality – but, most importantly, the body could be displayed without showing signs of violence: plausible deniability.

Richard II of England (died 1400)

Richard was deposed by Henry Bolingbroke (later Henry IV) in 1399, and confined first in the Tower of London and then in Pontefract Castle in Henry's Yorkshire powerbase. A plot by several disaffected earls to rescue Richard and assassinate Henry proved that the former king was too dangerous to live. What happened next remains unclear: various sources state that Richard either stopped eating, or was deliberately starved to death. Probably he died on 14 February. When his corpse was displayed in St Paul's Cathedral on 17 February, some remarked that it did not have the emaciated appearance typical of starvation: it is possible he was smothered to death.

George, Duke of Clarence (died 1478)

The younger brother of the Yorkist king Edward IV, George switched sides during the Wars of the Roses and was eventually convicted of treason and plotting to murder Edward IV. He was executed at the Tower of London, and although condemned nobles were usually beheaded, it is claimed that at his own request he was drowned in a butt of Malmsey wine. The story may even be true.

AD 1277

EDWARD I, HAMMER OF THE ~~SCOTS~~ WELSH

'I'm the King of the castle!'

The winning shout in a children's sandcastle game

The Welsh had obviously seen English armies before: mounted knights in chainmail, with archers and infantry, and with support services such as camp kitchens and armourers. But they had never seen anything like this: for travelling with the armed force were woodcutters and charcoal burners, quarrymen and roadbuilders, stonemasons and carpenters. The dense woodlands of North Wales, so long an effective barrier against invaders, were cut down; once an area was cleared, a castle was built; and once a castle was built, a supply port was constructed, and ships from the south coast of England appeared – and not just ships for cargo, but vessels capable of transporting troops, troops that could leapfrog around coastal strongpoints and strike at undefended cornfields behind the lines. The English were coming not just to win, but to overwhelm.

The architect of this vast exercise was Edward I, King of England and a warrior who knew that success in single battles might come from martial prowess, but actual wars were won by logistics and engineering. In later years Edward would be known as the Hammer of the Scots. But in 1277, Edward was embarking on another war: the total conquest of Wales.

Wales had never coalesced into a single unified kingdom like Scotland, probably because of its geography: the routes of communication did not run north-south within Wales itself, but east-west – directly into England. It was also far less populated and rich than its larger neighbour, and beset with inconvenient mountains. Maintaining law and order in such a terrain would be difficult. After 1066 the Norman solution was to set up buffer zones controlled by the Marcher Lords, whose vast estates in Cheshire, Shropshire and Herefordshire overlapped with the lowland parts of Wales. The Normans then worked their way through the coastal plain of South Wales, a route that attained greater importance when it became the invasion road for the colonisation of Dublin and eastern Ireland in the twelfth century. Everywhere the Normans went they built castles, and these castles became the foci of further inroads into the Welsh zone. In exchange for manning the frontline, the Marcher Lordships were granted unusual leeway: they were virtually mini kingdoms, where the lord's writ was far stronger than that of any king in far-away southern England. Not surprisingly, the barons were renowned for their cruelty and rapaciousness.

There were, of course, rebellions and resistance, and eventually North and central Wales became a semi-independent native power bloc. By the thirteenth century, the Llywelyn dynasty had carved out their own feudal kingdom, its political and economic structures the mirror image of feudal England. In 1267, after years of civil war in England during which the Welsh had made merry, Henry III of England pragmatically recognised Llywelyn ap Gruffydd as Prince of Wales. Five years later, however, Henry died – and his heir, Edward I, was dedicated to the cause of centralisation and a single, unitary state power. Welsh warlords behaving as if they were royal equals were simply untidy from an administrative point of view and would need to be dealt with. In 1276, Edward reinforced the border castles and gathered his forces. In 1277, he struck.

Three armies entered enemy territory through the coastal plains and river valleys, one in the west, one in mid-Wales, and one, led by Edward himself, in the North. Faced with a fait accompli, Llywelyn came to terms. He kept his title but had his lands greatly reduced. To enforce his will, Edward spent several years and vast sums building a ring of castles around Llywelyn's new border. He also started collecting taxes (never a popular move).

In 1282, a strong Welsh revolt achieved some early successes but Edward's castles now provided him with forward bases that enabled him to pin down the Welsh in their Snowdonia mountain fastness while simultaneously separating them from their breadbasket on the Isle of Anglesey. Llywelyn was killed in a skirmish and his brother David ended his life under the tender ministrations of Edward's torturers. Wales as an independent (or even semi-independent) principality was eclipsed, and for administrative purposes the country became part of England. With the revolt utterly quashed, Edward built three giant castles as guarantors of the peace: Caernarfon, Conwy and Harlech still stand today as masterworks of the

The often-repeated story that Edward wooed the Welsh by proclaiming his infant son as 'their' Welsh-born Prince of Wales and holding up the baby from the battlements of Caernarfon Castle to the cheers of the Welsh nobles is, by the way, just a myth. The tale was invented in the sixteenth century when the Welsh dynasty of the Tudors were on the throne and wished to newly glorify their ancestry. The fictional story is set at the time of the infant's birth in 1284, but young Prince Edward did not actually become Prince of Wales until 1301. Ever since that date, however, the eldest surviving son of the monarch has always been known as Prince of Wales, a tradition that continues with Prince Charles to this day.

The Seal of Edward I.

castle-builder's art. The immense and impressive Caernarfon was partly inspired by the great walls of imperial Byzantium, which gives an indication of the scale of Edward's ambitions.

A further revolt in 1294 led to Edward being besieged in his own castle at Conwy – and the walls held. Harlech too stood firm, but Caernarfon fell because its defensive circuit was still incomplete. After the revolt was put down with Edward's usual ruthless efficiency, he embarked on a third round of castle-building. Thanks to first the invading Normans, then the Marcher Lords, and finally the indefatigable manager-warrior Edward and his ring of iron, Wales is one of the most be-castled countries in the world, the fortresses bearing eloquent witness to centuries of strife.

AD 1314

THE BATTLE OF BANNOCKBURN

'Two hundred pairs of spurs all red
Were taken from the knights there dead.'

John Barbour, The Bruce, *1370s*

A fine summer's day in 1314. Early evening sunlight, the 'golden hour' beloved by film directors, adds a glowing lustre to the bucolic scene of field and stream, woodland and rolling pasture. Adding to the visual feast of the scene are a number of knights, champions all, bedecked in vivid surcoats and highly polished bascinets, sporting family crests on their brightly painted shields, their equally decorated mounts warhorses of the highest standard. We are looking at the very flower of chivalry.

The troupe cross a ford over a stream in a dip. Suddenly one rider gallops on ahead of the group. His name is Sir Henry de Bohun, and he has lived all his life in the hope of a perfect moment of chivalric honour, an act that will grant his name immortality.

The young man has seen a rider at the far treeline, a large man in a mailcoat with a leather cap over his bascinet. Surmounting the leather cap is a crown. This is Robert the Bruce, and Henry de Bohun is heading for glory, intending to kill the King of Scots in single combat and bring the battle to an end before it begins.

Bruce is riding a grey palfrey, a light saddle horse that is no match for de Bohun's tank-like steed. It would be prudent to withdraw, but a large part of the Scottish army is watching. Bruce sets spurs to his mount and rides directly at de Bohun as if it were a joust. The Englishman's lance misses. Bruce stands up in his stirrups and raises his battleaxe.

With a single blow he cleaves de Bohun's steel bascinet open and splits the skull in two. Such is the force of the thrust that the wooden shaft of the axe shatters.

The Scottish forces erupt with joy and surge forward, attacking the rest of the knights, many of whom are now unhorsed by camouflaged pits designed to break a horse's leg. The English retreat in confusion back over the ford. The first blood of the Battle of Bannockburn has gone to the Scots, and Bruce's almost superhuman feat is told around many a campfire that night.

Bannockburn was the climax of a long campaign waged by Robert the Bruce in the cause of an independent Scotland, an independence that had been threatened by Edward I's expansionist policies from 1295. Along the way, Bruce had waged a civil war against other Scots in pursuit of his right to wear the crown. He had murdered his principal rival, John 'the Red' Comyn, in front of the high altar of Greyfriars Church in Dumfries while under a flag of truce. He had burned and slaughtered his way across Galloway, Argyll, Buchan, Strathspey and parts of the Borders. Having disposed of or sidelined his domestic competitors, Bruce then mounted an increasingly effective guerrilla war

Edward's army were not just English. A number were Scots, typically supporters of the Comyn family (whose chief Bruce had treacherously murdered), and the nobles of the lands Bruce had ravaged.

Robert the Bruce about to split his rival's head in half.

against English occupation. The end result was a huge army coming north of the border, led by the new English king, Edward II, who was determined to relieve the English garrison besieged within the mighty rock-girt fortress of Stirling Castle. Well-informed by spies and turncoats of the route the English were taking, Bruce chose his battleground in advance, seeding it with traps and using marshy ground and valley-floor streams as defences. It was a brilliant tactic, and on the second day of the battle it worked like a dream.

The Battle of Bannockburn – Scottish pikemen versus English cavalry.

Bruce had had plenty of time to prepare. His infantry was finely drilled into 'schiltrons', porcupine-like clusters of spearmen whose pikes and spears formed an impenetrable barrier against the normally devastating heavy cavalry. With riderless horses and wounded and dying men getting in the way, the cavalry charges petered out. The hedges of spears advanced, penning the knights back towards the marshes and streams. As the English lines were pressed hard, another Scottish army appeared from behind a distant hill – although none of the English noticed that the waving banners of this new host were actually sheets tied to poles, for this was a ruse; another clever tactic by Bruce, who had had his camp followers and non-combatants camouflage themselves as reinforcements.

Edward II's finest were pushed back over the wetlands. So many corpses of horses and men choked the waterways that the pursuers could cross without getting their feet wet, and the streams themselves ran red. Some bodies sank without trace. The defeat became a rout, and the rout a disaster. Bruce had chosen his battlespace so ingeniously that many of the English infantrymen did not even get the chance to take part in the fight. Perhaps 200 of England's finest knights perished early in the battle, plus uncountable numbers of 'lesser folk', and many nobles were captured. Edward II himself was forced to ride for his life and took ship at Dunbar on the east coast.

It took another fourteen years from Bannockburn for England to formally recognise Scottish independence, but after Bruce died, his Scottish enemies renewed their claims, invading Scotland from England and prompting the Second War of Independence (1332–57).

Bruce and the Scottish army giving thanks after the victory at Bannockburn.

CRUEL AND UNUSUAL PUNISHMENTS

'I love to give pain.'

William Congreve, The Way of the World, *1700*

Kings, nobles and governments have over the centuries endeavoured to find novel ways to torment and humiliate both political prisoners and criminals who, it was felt, needed that little bit extra beyond the normal pleasures of the rope and the rack.

Encagement

In 1306, a Scottish supporter of Edward I of England captured several family members and friends of Robert the Bruce. While the men were hanged, drawn and beheaded, a different fate was in store for the women. Isobel of Fife, the Countess of Buchan, who had placed the crown on Bruce's head at his coronation at Scone, was confined to an iron cage placed out of doors on the walls of Berwick Castle. Other than the servant who brought her food and drink, she was forbidden to speak to anyone. Similarly, Mary Bruce, Robert's 24-year-old sister, was locked up in a cage suspended from Roxburgh Castle. Both women endured four years of what must have been appalling conditions – not to mention the 24/7 humiliation of being a public spectacle. They were moved to slightly more humane confinement in 1310 and exchanged for high-value English prisoners after the Battle of Bannockburn in 1314.

Drowning

Sometime before 975, a widow from Ailsworth near Peterborough was drowned at London Bridge for witchcraft (this was probably not the bridge in the capital, but a London Bridge somewhere local). As part of a property dispute she and her son had driven iron pins into a wax or wooden model of a landowner named Aelfsige – the son escaped and was outlawed but she was found in possession of the Anglo-Saxon equivalent of a voodoo doll, tried and condemned.

Staking and Crossroads Burial

In 1573, Thomas Maule from near Mansfield got drunk and hanged himself from a tree. He had to suffer the standard post-mortem punishment for suicides. His naked body was taken to a crossroads at midnight and thrown into a pit, and a wooden stake was driven through his chest. The lack of religious service and the burial outside consecrated ground ensured that his soul would not reach heaven, while the stake was there to prevent the body – animated by the Devil – rising and causing a nuisance. If the corpse did manage to struggle out of the ground, the multiple directions of the crossroads would confuse it further. The practice of burying at a crossroads was outlawed by Parliament in 1823, but things change slowly in the countryside, and a suicide named Oram was interred at the four-ways of Maddington in Wiltshire as late as 1849.

Mutilation and Amputation

The law codes of Henry II specified that petty larceny (stealing items worth less than a shilling) was to be punished by the cutting off of an ear. If the criminal repeated his offence he lost the other ear, and, in an early 'three strikes and you're out' ordinance, the third crime led to the gallows. Theft of items of value greater than a shilling resulted in a progressively higher loss of flesh and bone: first a thumb, then a hand, and finally a foot.

Boiling to Death

This revolting execution method was first instigated in 1531 by Henry VIII, and is unusual in that it was a knee-jerk reaction to a specific case of poisoning, and indeed the very culprit is named in the Act itself. Richard Roose, a cook, cast poison into the yeast in the kitchens of the Bishop of Rochester's palace at Lambeth. Two people died and fifteen others sickened, but the intended target – the bishop – did not eat the porridge. The attempted murder of the ecclesiastic was deemed high treason, and boiling to death was thereafter decreed as the legal punishment for poisoners. Roose was boiled alive in a metal vessel at Smithfield in London on 15 April, and the same site also saw the boiling of maidservant Mary Davy in 1542 for poisoning members of her household. Another servant poisoner suffered the same fate in King's Lynn. These are the only three cases where

the punishment was enacted, and boiling poisoners to death ceased with a change of the law in 1547.

Hanging in chains

This was a post-mortem punishment designed to publically exhibit the body for months, if not years. The first example on record is from Easthampstead in Berkshire in 1381, when Richard II ordered that some miscreants be not cut down from the gallows, but displayed in purpose-built chains as a warning to others. For the next four centuries hanging in chains, or 'gibbeting' was used sporadically against murderers guilty of particularly heinous crimes, as well as pirates. In 1752, gibbeting became for the first time a standard part of the sentence for murder, and the process became industrialised: the man was measured for his chains while still alive, and after the execution the body was thrown into a cauldron of boiling pitch to preserve the flesh. When the pitch had cooled, the corpse was packed in cold-riveted chains that, in their most elaborate form, resembled an iron exoskeleton. The last murderer to be hung in made-to-measure chains was gibbeted at Leicester in 1834.

Pressing to Death

First coming into use in 1406, this was originally a form of persuasion rather than execution. Unless an accused person pled 'guilty' or 'not guilty', a trial in England could not legally go ahead. In addition, if a man was found guilty and condemned to death, the Crown seized all his property. Many defendants therefore said nothing, hoping either to cause the prosecution to be abandoned, or preferring to die without sentence so that their property would remain with their heirs

and families. Pressing, or *peine forte et dure* ('strong and hard punishment/pain'), was first used to induce such men to plead, although eventually it became a way of removing uncooperative individuals. The victim was laid on his back with his limbs extended, and heavier and heavier weights then placed on his chest and abdomen. At some point most men of course gave in, and agreed to plead, but a few held out. In 1685, for example, Major George Strangeways refused to plead on the charge of murdering his brother-in-law, and was ordered to be pressed. He arranged for his friends to lie on top of the weights so as to speed his death: after some ten minutes of dreadful lung-crushing and stomach-rupturing agony he expired, having been convicted of no crime and hence successfully preventing the state from seizing his family property.

Heads on Stakes

The credit for introducing medieval London to the public display of hacked-off heads lies with King Edward I, who was an innovator not just in warfare but also in the associated public relations campaigns. The first head on display belonged to Llywelyn, Prince of Wales, whom Edward had finally defeated in 1282. It was contemptuously crowned with ivy, and set up on the highest turret of the Tower of London. The following year it was joined by that of Llywelyn's brother David. The Tower, however, although symbolic, was simply too tall – you had to squint far up to look at the heads grinning down at you.

'Pressing' in action.

The next head of a vanquished enemy was therefore set up somewhere much more public and accessible: London Bridge. The victim was William Wallace, victor of the Battle of Stirling Bridge and hero of the Scottish resistance against Edward the Hammer. This is how Matthew of Westminster described Wallace's 'amply deserved' death:

> First he was led through the streets of London, dragged at the tail of a horse, to a very high gallows, made on purpose for him, where he was hanged with a halter; then taken down half dead, after which his genitals were cut off, and his body divided into four quarters, and his head fixed on a stake and set on London Bridge. But his four quarters thus divided were sent to the four quarters of Scotland.

Some revolting peasants. Note the severed heads on pikes.

The heads of traitors, rebels and political enemies were periodically displayed in London for more than another 500 years.

A corpse hanged, drawn and quartered.

THE BLACK DEATH

'Nature, the vicar of the Almighty Lord.'

Geoffrey Chaucer, 'The Parliament of Fowls', written around 1380

In 1349, the Scots, encouraged by reports that their southern neighbour was being destabilised by a mysterious disease, invaded northern England. This decision is a candidate for the worst military idea ever – for the mysterious disease was none other than the Black Death, the most virulent epidemic in history. Within a short time 5,000 men of the Scottish army were dead from the disease. The rest dispersed, taking the plague with them back to their villages and farms. The following year, the deadly bacteria were at play in the fields of Scotland. 'So great a plague has never been heard of from the beginning of the world,' wrote the Scottish chronicler John of Fordun, adding, 'fully a third of the human race was killed.'

If the Black Death had been a rock group, then the T-shirt for the 1348–50 European Tour would have listed an impressive catalogue of venues, from Italy, France, Flanders and Spain to Scandinavia, Iceland and even Greenland. The Black Death arrived in the British Isles in June 1348, making landfall with European sailors in Dorset. By August it had reached Bristol, then England's second or third largest town. In September, mass plague pits were being hastily dug in an overwhelmed London. By the autumn of 1349, the 'great mortality' had devastated Wales, Ireland and most of England. It was at this point that the Scots decided to invade. In truth, the plague would have reached Scotland eventually, but the way its infected army scattered through the kingdom hastened and arguably exacerbated the spread of the dread pestilence.

Perhaps 30 to 45 per cent of the total population of the British Isles perished between 1348 and 1350 – somewhere in the region of 2 million people. The worst visitation was in East Anglia, where the general mortality was 50 per cent, with some villages suffering losses as high as 60 or even 70 per cent. Everywhere, many older and high-status people died: in some areas, estate administration and the justice system collapsed. Mills no longer ground. Bread went unbaked. Thousands of cattle died from lack of care and not being milked. The dead remained unburied.

The death rates were higher for some specific populations, such as priests and monks who

The Black Death and subsequent epidemics inspired the iconography of 'The Dance of Death,' where King Death, represented as a skeleton, appears to everyone from kings and queens to priests and bishops. This series is from a nineteenth-century reworking.

attended the sick. So many people were dying and there were so few priests that the majority of the infected perished without having made confession – which, in the universal Catholic belief of the time, severely imperilled their entry into heaven. The Bishop of Bath and Wells therefore granted permission for dying laymen to make confession among themselves – and, as an absolute last resort, if no one else was available, to a woman. This dispensation alone revealed just how much the certainties of the medieval world were unravelling under the pressure of 'God's scythe'.

The disease was initially blood-borne, injected into the bodies of humans by the bite of rat-launched fleas, causing the infected lymph nodes to swell into the characteristic 'buboes' at armpit and groin – the bubonic plague. The bacillus could also be inhaled – the pneumonic plague – leading to the victim howking up bloody sputum that was itself a vector for further contamination of others. In every case decline was painful, swift (one to four days) and fatal. A damp climate also tended to increase pulmonary complications – the colder and wetter your life, the more at risk you were – while the pneumonic plague loved nothing better than the vile sanitary conditions in the towns.

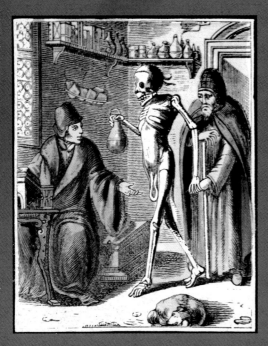

The Black Death was not a static disease, the bacillus mutating as new hosts and new environments presented new opportunities. In the winter of 1349–50, for example, its progress further north was checked by the Scottish winter, but the spring of 1350 saw the disease return with a vengeance. There also seemed to have been several variants, whose cross-spread may have further exacerbated the virulence: East Anglia was almost certainly first infected via ships from the Netherlands. A different strain then arrived from London, and the combination of the two probably accounted for the area's extraordinary degree of plague morbidity, one of the highest levels in the whole of Europe.

If the 1348–50 visitation was bad enough, the long-term effects were made worse by the return of the plague in 1361–64. In the interim, many people widowed during the first plague had got married and raised children, so the overall population was starting to recover. The death rates in 1361 were lower – but this time around, the pestilence was known specifically as the 'mortality of children'. Large numbers of children never reached maturity and hence never reproduced, with an ongoing impact on the population that was exacerbated by further age-specific epidemics in 1368–69 and the early 1370s. By the end of the fourteenth century the population of England had halved.

We have, in recent years, fallen rather awkwardly in love with the notion of 'the apocalypse', a theme

that runs through both science fiction and religious 'end of days' paranoia. For some people in the fourteenth century, the Black Death appeared as a veritable apocalypse, a real-life end of the world. In Kilkenny, Brother John Clyn, an Irish Minorite Friar, left a note of the events destined for a future generation – if indeed there were to be future generations: 'That the writing may not perish with the scribe, or the work fail with the labourer, I add parchment to continue it, if by chance anyone may be left in the future, and any son of Adam may escape this pestilence and continue the work thus begun.' The next line is in different handwriting: 'Here it seems that the author died.'

When it comes to mass death, war is a mere beginner when compared to Mother Nature.

OWAIN GLYNDWR: WALES IN REVOLT

'Strange wonders happened (as men reported) at the nativity of this man, for the same night he was born, all his father's horses in the stable were found to stand in blood up to their bellies.'

Raphael Holinshed, Chronicles of England, Scotland and Ireland, 1587

A portrait of Owain Glyndwr based on his seal.

Sometimes wars break out for the most trivial of reasons. In 1400, a minor Welsh landowner named Owain Glyndwr had a boundary dispute with his neighbour, the immensely powerful Marcher Lord Reginald Grey of Ruthin. The spat descended into small-scale violence, then escalated into skirmishing – and within a short time, a full-scale insurrection was underway. There were stories of Welsh clerks abandoning their jobs in London to travel home to join the uprising, while Welsh students at Oxford and Welsh labourers on English farms were doing the same thing. Popular enthusiasm equated Glyndwr with the heroes of old, those of whom the bards still sang.

Glyndwr himself was an unlikely hero. In his mid-40s, he had been a court official in London before settling down to comfortable obscurity in North Wales. He did, however, have two advantages: he was descended from ancient Welsh royalty, a key element for a people dedicated to genealogy and lineage; and he had the charisma of a born leader. In the first year of the revolt he may well have called the whole thing off had his property disputes been resolved in his favour. As it was, he was branded a traitor by the Crown, and his response was both tumultuous and revolutionary. At the peak of his power he was the *de facto* ruler of the entire Welsh nation, was crowned Prince of Wales, and made plans to set up institutions such as an independent Welsh Church, two universities, a parliament and a civil service. Glyndwr had started as a warrior focused on a local grievance, but now his ambition was nothing less than a unified, independent Welsh kingdom, something never before seen.

Starting in 1400, Glyndwr's campaign saw both victories and setbacks, but the times were in his favour. His campaign was centred on avoiding pitched battles with the numerically superior English forces. Instead he concentrated on both guerrilla warfare and short, sharp attacks on individual castles.

In 1401, Glyndwr was joined by one the great Marcher Lords, the alliance punching a hole in the buffer zone between the Welsh mountain fastness and the English lowlands. By 1403 he was receiving assistance from France, with French ships assaulting English castles at Caernarfon and Anglesey. In 1405, a French expedition landed at Milford Haven and attacked Haverfordwest, Tenby and Carmarthen.

The same year, which saw the height of Glyndwr's power, an extraordinary tripartite document was drawn up between three foes of Henry IV: once they disposed of the king, Glyndwr was to have the whole of Wales and the Marcher Lands from the Severn and Worcester to the Mersey; the Earl of Northumberland was to take control of the North and Midlands; and Edmund Mortimer, who had a claim to the English throne, was granted southern England. As it was, these grand designs came to naught. English armies were initially hampered by long and vulnerable supply lines, atrocious weather and the difficulties posed by the mountainous geography. But by 1406–07, the tide had turned: English military successes gradually boxed Glyndwr in, and by 1410 he had virtually disappeared. He may have died in around 1415 or 1417, though the location of his grave is unknown. Several of his confederates became outlaws, achieving a kind of Robin Hood-like local fame, while Wales as a whole

It was not until the reign of Henry VIII and the Acts of Union of 1536 and 1543 that Wales became fully part of the centralised state apparatus based in London. For the first time, Welsh people, who had until now been second-class citizens, now achieved full equality before the law. The legal and local government systems were standardised. There was one inevitable consequence of this centralisation: the extensive decline of the Welsh language and the imposition of an Anglo-centric culture, especially in South Wales.

descended into lawlessness and disorder. Many Welshmen went on to fight in the wars in France and then in the Wars of the Roses – and when they returned home, skilled in all the arts of plunder and pillage, more chaos ensued.

AD 1415

HENRY V – AGINCOURT AND ALL THAT

'Once more unto the breach, dear friends, once more;
Or close the wall up with our English dead.'

Henry V at the Siege of Harfleur, according to Shakespeare in Henry V

The blacksmith was half dead when the prince ordered the flames to be extinguished. Shielding his nose against the smell of burned flesh, the king's eldest son approached and offered a pardon and a pension for life if the man would renounce his heresy, and agree that the Holy Sacrament was not merely a piece of bread but indeed the veritable Body of Christ. When the blacksmith refused to recant, the faggots around the stake at Smithfield were relit and young Prince Henry calmly watched as the wretched man died in agony.

The French garrison at Rouen opened the gates of their besieged city and drove out 12,000 'useless' women, children, invalids and old men who could not fight. It was the depths of winter. His Most Gracious and Sovereign Majesty King Henry V refused the non-combatants permission to pass through the English lines, and, trapped between the city walls and the unyielding besiegers, all 12,000 died of exposure and starvation.

These are perhaps not the stories you associate with Henry V, one of the great hero-kings of

English history. After all, Henry was the winner at the Battle of Agincourt in 1415, a crushing victory over numerically superior French forces that still casts its mythological shadow over British politics and popular sentiment today, largely because of the stirring words Shakespeare put into Henry's mouth nearly 200 years after the battle:

We few, we happy few, we band of brothers;
For he to-day that sheds his blood with me
Shall be my brother; be he ne'er so vile,
This day shall gentle his condition;
And gentlemen in England now-a-bed
Shall think themselves accurs'd they were
    not here,
And hold their manhoods cheap whiles
    any speaks
That fought with us upon Saint Crispin's day.

Yet Henry was far more complex a character than even Shakespeare could portray. A great-grandson of Edward III, at his birth he was as far from the

65

throne as it was possible for an aristocrat to be – yet by the time he was 12, his father had usurped the kingdom and Henry was next in line for the throne. Henry's experience of a turbulent and violently unstable England (not to mention Wales, Ireland and Scotland) shaped his two abiding pragmatic principles: rule by whatever means necessary; and rule to win. Thus, if he could achieve his goals by being generous or merciful, then generosity and

An eerily semi-mystical view of Henry V the warrior.

mercy would be offered. But if an iron fist was required – well, then it was time for pitiless brutality.

Henry became king in 1413, at the age of 25. Two years later, he embarked on the great adventure of his reign – war against France, an activity which occupied him for the rest of his short life. An able administrator and organiser, Henry's war was well bankrolled, well resourced, and even – courtesy of taxes, fines and ransoms collected from his newly conquered territories – profitable,

Portrait of Henry V – a side view to hide the scarring caused by the arrow that struck him in the face at the Battle of Shrewsbury. (LOC, LC-USZ62-112536)

and therefore popular. The truly amazing victory at Agincourt during the first campaign – which saw the extinction of much of the French nobility – was the icing on the cake. For the next seven years Henry's troops cut a bloody swathe across northern France.

And so it was that in the winter of 1418–19, after four months of siege, with the population reduced to eating cats, mice, old leather and shoes, the French garrison at Rouen cast out its 'useless mouths'. The English troops, usually inured to every horror of war, were so appalled at the sight of the hordes of walking skeletons that they offered them their own bread. Henry immediately put a stop to that, and both sides watched as first dozens, and then hundreds, of the evacuees died each day of cold and hunger in the no-man's-land between the city fortifications and the English siege lines. When one woman gave birth, the baby was winched up in a basket to a priest waiting on the walls: he baptised the infant, then returned it to its mother, with a benediction to die well in the love of Christ. Three weeks later, when it was obvious that the long-awaited relieving army would not be coming, the Rouen garrison, starved into submission, finally surrendered. In contrast to the siege of Caen in 1417, when the defeated residents suffered the unrelenting bloodlust of Henry's murderous troops, Rouen was not put to the sack – Henry, pragmatic as ever, needed it intact as an administrative centre for his continuing campaign.

As for the man burned at the stake, his name was John Badby. He was a Lollard, a loosely knit group who were inspired by the recent translation of the Bible into English to seek limited reforms of the Catholic Church. Amongst other things, they denied the Transubstantiation, the belief that the wine and host of the Holy Communion were literally transubstantiated into the Blood and Body of Christ. Declared heretics by the Church, Lollards were persecuted and burned at the stake. In 1410, Badby became the first layman executed in England for heresy. In 1413 Sir John Oldcastle, one of the king's oldest friends, became another Lollard martyr. Long before Bloody Mary and her notorious burning times, Englishmen were being burned for simply believing in a form of religion at slight variance to that preached by those in power. And among that power elite was Henry V – a pious, deeply religious king who went on pilgrimages and gave generously to ecclesiastical establishments. In burning those condemned as heretics, Henry was in a way only doing his job as defender of the Catholic Church.

Rule by whatever means necessary; and rule to win.

SEX, LIES AND WITCHCRAFT

'Ah, gracious lord, these days are dangerous: Virtue is choked with foul ambition.'

The Duke of Gloucester in Shakespeare's Henry VI, *Part 2*

King Henry V died in 1422, aged just 35. His son and heir, Henry VI, was only 9 months old at the time, so the late king's two brothers were appointed to rule until the boy attained his majority. The eldest brother and senior regent, John, the Duke of Bedford, pursued the ongoing Hundred Years' War in France, while the younger sibling, Humphrey, the Duke of Gloucester, as Protector of the Realm, was responsible for administration back in England. John died in 1435, when his nephew Henry VI was 14 years old; if the teenage monarch died without children, Humphrey would be the next King of England. Opposing Humphrey was his powerful half-uncle, Cardinal Beaufort, who sought not only to increase his own influence over the young king, but to eliminate the Duke of Gloucester from the succession altogether.

Humphrey was a highly educated and cultured man who had fought well in the French wars. He had one obvious vulnerability though: his second wife, Eleanor Cobham. Eleanor had first entered the duke's bed at the age of 25, and three years later, once Gloucester's first marriage had been annulled, she became his wife. Eleanor was the daughter of a knight, which in modern terms placed her somewhere in the middle of the middle class; in 1436, the one-time mistress and lady-in-waiting was elevated to the position of Duchess of Gloucester – the commoner had become aristocracy, an astonishing event for medieval England. In addition, her husband was now first in line to the throne – and beautiful, strong-minded and intelligent Eleanor started to think she might one day become queen. Her pride made enemies.

In early 1440, Eleanor started to dabble in the occult: she wished to see into the future, to divine how long Henry VI would live, and thus know whether her husband would ever become king. To this end she consulted three scholars: Master Roger Bolingbroke, a priest, Oxford graduate and her personal clerk; Master Thomas Southwell, canon of St Stephen's chapel in the Palace of Westminster, rector of St Stephen's at Walbrook in London, and vicar of Ruislip in Middlesex; and her chaplain and secretary, John Home, canon of Hereford and St Asaph. All three had the knowledge of Latin necessary to read old tomes on astrology, divination and magic. In addition, Eleanor employed the services of Margery Jourdemayne, a 'witch' from Eye near Westminster, who specialised in love potions and other intimate charms: Eleanor was now 40, and desperate to conceive a child.

In the summer of 1441, the storm broke. Margery and the three men were arrested, accused of conspiring to cause the king's death. Bolingbroke was supposedly a necromancer; Southwell had allegedly blessed the magical instruments at a blasphemous Mass; and Home was their accomplice. Eleanor, the Duchess of Gloucester, one of the most powerful women in the land, immediately launched herself into the temporary safety of the religious sanctuary at Westminster Abbey.

Bolingbroke may have been tortured: certainly he soon named Eleanor as his patroness. Dressed in his magical robes and surrounded by his occult tools, Bolingbroke publically confessed his crimes to a large audience of powerful and influential men. The way was now clear for the prosecution of the duchess, something her husband was powerless to prevent. It was claimed that the magical group had invoked demons and evil spirits, and fashioned a wax image of Henry VI that was 'dwindled' to cause the king's death. Faced with twenty-eight counts of treason and witchcraft, Eleanor confessed to five charges. Her husband's political enemies had won.

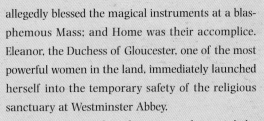

Westminster Abbey, where the
Duchess of Gloucester took sanctuary.
(LOC, LC-DIG-ppmsc-08570)

Margery, the 'Witch of Eye', was burned at the stake. Thomas Southwell died in the Tower of London; knowing the dreadful punishment that awaited convicted necromancers, he may well have taken poison. Roger Bolingbroke was not so lucky: he was dragged behind a horse from the Tower to the execution site at Tyburn, and then hanged, disembowelled while still alive, his head cut off to decorate London Bridge, and the four quarters of his body sent to be displayed in Oxford, Cambridge and two other towns as a warning to young intellectual clerks about the dangers of heretical thinking about magic. John Home, who only had an incidental supporting role, was pardoned.

As for Eleanor, she was first forcibly divorced from her husband, made to perform humiliating public penances during three busy London market days, and was then incarcerated for the rest of her life.

Kenilworth Castle, Eleanor's first prison.
(LOC, LC-DIG-ppmsc-08469)

Her first residences were the castles of Chester and Kenilworth, but as rumours of plots to free her circulated with increasing frequency, more distant quarters were required, and she was transferred to Peel Castle on the Isle of Man. After the trial, Humphrey was a broken man politically, and he died in 1447, a few days after himself being arrested for treason. Eleanor, still in prison, outlived him by a decade.

The dreaded Tower of London, where Bolingbroke, the Duke of Clarence and Anne Boleyn all perished. (LC-DIG-ppmsc-08566)

'Ordeal: Old English ordël, 'judgement'.'

Brewer's Dictionary of Phrase & Fable, *1999 edition*

Crime, trial, punishment and death are always with us. Here are some of the less pleasant ways British men and women have tangled with the law and with custom.

Blunt force trauma, strangulation, exsanguination

Discovered in a peat bog in Cheshire in 1984, the well-preserved 'bog body' of Lindow Man dates to around 300 BC and is on display at the British Museum. The man had been bludgeoned on the back of the head with a heavy object, garrotted, and had his throat cut, before being left below the waterline in a marshy environment. The ritualistic nature of the 'triple death', plus other clues from analysis of his last meal, skin and hair, suggests that almost certainly he was a victim of human sacrifice by the Druids, and that he was probably nobly born, and may even have been a volunteer. Perhaps some crisis needed to be averted and the gods could only be placated with a sacrifice of the highest order.

Castration

Matthew Paris, a monk based at St Albans, left an invaluable chronicle of his time. Here is an extract from 1248:

A certain Norfolk Knight of noble birth and accomplished prowess, named Godfrey de Millers ... one night secretly entered the house of a knight called John Brito to sleep with his daughter. But he was prevented by some people placed in ambush with the contrivance of the whore ... He was seized, savagely thrown to the ground and badly wounded. Then he was suspended from a beam by his feet with his legs stretched apart, so that he was completely at the mercy of his enemies, who disgracefully mutilated him by cutting off his genital organs, though he would have preferred to be beheaded ... he was thrown out half dead.

Astonishingly, Godfrey survived, and brought a case against John Brito, who was deprived of his property and exiled for life. Other family members were banished, and the woman avoided the death penalty by going into hiding. 'This inhuman and in every way merciless crime,' lamented Paris, 'involved many nobles in an miserable calamity.'

Hanged by the Neck Until Ye Be Dead

In 1819 a Member of Parliament, Fowell Buxton, researched the legal archives and estimated that, as the law stood, no less than 223 crimes were

The famous Hogarth view of a London execution, with the Triple Tree in the background.

punishable by death. These included not just the most serious offences – murder, treason, piracy, arson and rape – but such bizarre actions as: making a false entry in the financial records of the Bank of England; damaging Westminster Bridge; assaulting a Privy Councillor; signing a demand for money under a false name; escaping from quarantine; and impersonating a Chelsea Pensioner. The crime of most executed criminals was actually theft, and many who perished at the end of a rope were children: in 1808 two sisters in Lynn were sentenced to death for robbery – they were aged 11 and 8.

Trial by Ordeal

The Laws of Wihtred, king of the Anglo-Saxons of Kent, were issued in 695, and provide a clear insight into the way justice was administered in a culture that had been Christian for only a century: basically, in difficult cases, God had to decide who was guilty. In front of an assembly known as a folk-moot (or, later, a court), the accused swore a great and holy oath that he was innocent. 'Oath-helpers' also swore

in his favour, and the more oath-helpers there were and the more powerful they were, then the greater the likelihood that the accused would be acquitted. If he was found guilty, however, he had two choices. The first was to pay the fine (and Anglo-Saxon society had set monetary values on every form of infraction, from theft to murder, and every man had his wirgild or 'life-gold' value). The second option was to apply to the only Appeal Court available: the ordeal. Trial by ordeal came in three forms. The first was to be bound and thrown into a pool (if you were innocent, you floated). The second was to plunge your hand into boiling water and retrieve a stone; if you were accused of one crime, the water was wrist deep – three counts, however, meant the water would reach to your elbow. The third ordeal was that of fire. A red-hot bar of iron was removed from the fire with tongs and placed on a wooden post. The accused then had to pick up the bar with his bare hand and walk 9ft. In both the latter cases, the scalded or burned hand was bound in a clean bandage; if after three days the wound had healed, God had clearly judged the accused to be innocent. Suppurating sores, however, marked the sufferer down as guilty by divine pronouncement, and so the fine would still have to be paid.

Choked with cheese

In a refinement of the Anglo-Saxon ordeal procedure, men of the Church who were accused of crimes were force-fed bread or cheese. If they choked on it they were clearly guilty – because the food had been consecrated in advance, and so only those with evil in their hearts could reject such a holy repast.

AD 1455

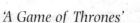

THE WARS OF THE ROSES

'A Game of Thrones'

Title of a novel by George R.R. Martin, 1996

'You're watching The Wars of the Roses – Live! And welcome viewers to what they're already calling the game of the century – the fifteenth century that is. Stuart?'

'You're absolutely right, Barry, this is going to be a scorcher of a match, with two sides evenly matched, the lads from the House of York bearing their white roses, and their blood rivals from the House of Lancaster tricked out in their brand new red livery. We're expecting both teams to give a hundred and ten per cent.'

'Absolutely Stuart. And you can be assured that we're going to be following every battle, foul murder and piece of treachery in this vicious civil war. Don't expect any fair play here. And we fully anticipate mass casualties not just among the players, but among their supporters as well. While we're waiting for things to kick off, Stuart, for the viewers at home who've just joined us, can you just give us a bit of background on this particular grudge match?'

'Can do, Barry. The House of Lancaster have been on the throne since 1399, ever since Henry Bolingbroke deposed his cousin Richard II and

Micklegate Bar. Richard's head was placed on top between AD 1440 and 1441. Other famous heads to decorate the Bar include Percy 'Hotspur', Lord Scrope, the Earls of Devon and Northumberland and several Jacobites. (LOC, LC-DIG-ppmsc-09038)

became Henry IV. Then you get Henry V, no problem there, good lad when it comes to getting stuck in, but along comes Henry VI, not the strongest of kings, and now you've got Richard Duke of York trying to take the crown from the Lancastrians – '

'I have to interrupt you there Stuart, because it's now 1455 and it looks likes things are about to kick off – yes, it's the Battle of St Albans, but it's a nil-nil draw, both sides retiring to lick their wounds for a few years – and oh! – the Yorkists have captured Henry VI at the Battle of Northampton! He must be sick as a parrot!'

'Ah, but don't count your chickens Barry, because Richard Duke of York has been killed at the Battle of Wakefield! The Lancastrians have got Henry VI back!'

'That's as may be, Stuart, but look at that – the Yorkists have won the Battle of Towton. The White Rose boys are back on top and their striker Edward IV is now king!'

'Well, yes, but I detect some problems in the York team, Barry. The Earl of Warwick seems to be up to something. Yes, I can hear the crowd chanting his nickname – 'Kingmaker! Kingmaker!' The midfield maestro seems to be trying to replace Edward with the king's own brother, George. No, wait, that little ploy has run its course, and now – blimey! – Warwick seems to have changed sides! He's now supporting the deposed Henry VI!'

'And now the game is just ping-ponging back and forth between one half of the pitch and the

An imaginative view of the death of the princes in the Tower.

other, Stuart. Look at the way each side's fortunes are changing!'

'But watch out, here comes Edward IV striking deep into enemy territory. For a big lad, he's good with his feet. He's killed the Earl of Warwick! He's killed the Prince of Wales, the Lancastrian heir! And he's killed Henry VI! The Lancaster team have no more contenders! The Yorkists are triumphant!'

'And as the half-time whistle blows at 1471, Stuart, what are your thoughts?'

'Well Barry, it's been a tough, hard-fought first half, lots of major battles, lots of team members selling out their own side, but at the end of the day it's bums on thrones that counts, and I have to say at this point in time that it looks like the House of York have set out their stall and have really got their mojo working on that end of things.'

'Well Stuart, I always say it's a game of two halves. And now the whistle's blown for the resumption of hostilities, and I've just been informed that Edward IV has died. Bit of a shock there for the York camp, I think, even if it is 1483. So now it looks like his son Edward V is king, but he's just a boy, so who's going to be the real captain? – Ah, here we go, it's Edward IV's younger brother, that Richard of Gloucester fellow. The Crooked Duke, they call him.'

'Allegedly, Barry.'

'Yes, Stuart, allegedly.'

'So is the winter of discontent going to be made glorious summer by this son of York?'

'Search me, Stuart.'

'Barry, over there in the Tower of London, can you see? The 12-year-old Edward V is in captivity, along with his younger brother. And their uncle Richard of Gloucester is looking a bit shifty.'

'Sorry, Stuart, there's a lot of dust and smoke being kicked up, it's obscuring what's really happening ... wait, something's becoming clear – yes, Richard of Gloucester has the crown! Richard III is now the next Yorkist King of England!'

'Er, what about the princes in the Tower, Barry?'

'Sorry mate, don't know exactly, but I'm pretty sure they won't be needing any more birthday candles, if you see what I mean.'

'I do, Barry, I do. Wait, who's that new player on the field?'

'The information's just coming in now ... apparently he's a distant descendant of the House of Lancaster, a chap named Henry Tudor.'

'So the Lancastrians are back on the pitch! There's everything to play for!'

'Stuart, the two sides are facing up to each other at a place called Bosworth Field. Richard III has the larger army, but there seems to be some problems with communication on the field ... he's decided to bring things to a quick end by charging straight at Henry Tudor – he's hacking his way through – but he's blocked, he's blocked, he can't get at his opposite number, he's forced back on the defensive, ah, he's lost his horse – and, oh, oh, Richard III is dead! Stuart, the Yorkist king Richard III is dead! Henry Tudor has been proclaimed King Henry VII!'

'You're right, Barry. Some people are on the pitch. They think it's all over ... it is now.'

PRETENDERS TO THE THRONE

'Dear body of Christ, I am bored with insurrection!'

Henry VII in the BBC TV series The Shadow of the Tower, *1972*

HENRY VII

There's a reason why we continue to be fascinated with the Tudors. It's not just Henry VIII's six wives, or Elizabeth I as the Virgin Queen. It's not just the sexual intrigues, or the plots and counterplots, or the executions, or major events such as the Reformation or the defeat of the Spanish Armada. It's because the Tudors raised England's game, forever.

Before the first Tudor king, Henry VII, came to the throne in 1485, England was an impoverished and insignificant kingdom, its earlier might dispersed by an internal civil war that had bled the country dry, as the white rose of York and the red rose of Lancaster jockeyed for the throne.

In just twenty-four years there had been six kings, two of them victims of murder. And yet when the last Tudor monarch, Elizabeth, passed away in 1603, England was a great military and sea power, a cultural powerhouse wealthy with trade, secure from enemies, and with a stable economy and administration. In 118 years, the Tudors had transformed England from a backwater into a great nation with a global destiny. Their successors, the Stuarts, look like a bit of a shower in comparison.

When the royal circlet was placed on his head amidst the bloodbath of Bosworth Field, the 28-year-old Henry Tudor, scion of the House of

Lancaster, was faced with an uphill task. In a brilliant series of political and judicial manoeuvres, Henry took on his over-mighty nobles and salted them for every penny he could take. He created a personal royal bodyguard, the Yeomen of the Guard, whose red-liveried successors still patrol the Tower of London. And he started to build up the fortunes of the Crown. Henry intended to restore the dignity of the office of king – and to do that, he needed to be not only the most powerful man in the kingdom, but also the wealthiest.

But there were still challenges to Henry's rule from the defeated Yorkists – notably the youthful Earl of Warwick, Edward IV's nephew and son of the Duke of Clarence (the man famous for having been drowned in a butt of malmsey wine). The young earl was banged up in the Tower of London. This in turn created a truly bizarre episode: the rise of the pretender to the throne, Lambert Simnel.

Simnel was the son of an Oxford tradesman – but he looked just like the earl. Edward IV's sister and her allies took the 10-year-old boy, crowned 'King Edward VI' in Dublin, and placed him at the head of an invasion force that landed on the coast of Lancashire on 4 June 1487. At the army's core were some 2,000 hardened mercenaries from Germany and Switzerland. Over the next ten days, the Yorkists fought and won a series of minor victories over the forces loyal to Henry VII. But then, on 15 June, the full might of the royal army congregated at Stoke Field, in Nottinghamshire, and faced off against the invaders.

The Battle of Stoke Field has largely been forgotten, although the numbers involved were larger than at the Battle of Bosworth two years earlier, and many more men were killed. Despite the European mercenaries being armed with the very latest military technology – handguns – after three hours of butchery, the fake earl's army was defeated by Henry's long-distance artillery: his archers. Annihilated by the sky-darkening rains of arrows, the Yorkists broke and ran, many being cut down in a place still known today as the Bloody Gutter. Perhaps 4,000 men – half the Yorkist army – died that day. The mercenaries fought to the last man: their corpses were found peppered with up to a dozen arrows apiece.

All of the Yorkist commanders perished, including the Earl of Lincoln. Lambert Simnel, however, survived. Rather than make a martyr out of him, Henry put the lad to work in the bowels of the royal household: overnight, Simnel went from a crowned king to a kitchen skivvy.

If one lookalike pretender to the throne wasn't enough, in 1491 a second arrived: Perkin Warbeck. Warbeck was hailed in France and Flanders as the real Richard, Duke of York, one of the two 'Princes in the Tower' who had probably been murdered in the Tower of London by Richard III. Warbeck, a commoner who knew a good thing when he saw it, enjoyed a charmed life in various European courts for several years. In 1495 he sailed to Scotland, where James IV recognised him as the true King of England and delighted in showing off his 'royal' guest. Two years later, a rebellion broke

Lambert Simnel in the royal kitchens.

out in Cornwall, and Warbeck decided to throw in his lot with the Cornishmen. When the revolt was crushed – very bloodily – Warbeck was captured.

As before, Henry was merciful, and the pretender was only placed in confinement. However, in 1499, a plot was uncovered that was designed to break out not only Warbeck, but also the real Earl of Warwick, who had been incarcerated in the Tower for fourteen years. Both men were summarily executed. There were no further Yorkist plots.

THE SIX EXECUTIONS OF HENRY VIII

'Exterminate!'

The Daleks, 1964

The life of Henry VIII is usually told in terms of his six wives. Here, in contrast, is his story told as six executions. Each of the murders reveals something of Henry's mercurial and ruthless personality.

'I'm 'Enery the Eighth, I am.'

1. THE EARL OF SUFFOLK (1513)

Henry VII promised not to harm the brother of the Earl of Lincoln – the one who died at Stoke Field. Instead, he was to be imprisoned for life. Henry VIII had no such compunction. In 1513 he was about to embark for war in France, and he feared his absence would give the Yorkists an excuse for rebellion. He promptly had the 40-year-old earl beheaded, just in case.

2. SIR THOMAS MORE (1535)

Henry's advisors tended to have a high attrition rate. In order to divorce his wife, Henry split from Rome and declared himself head of the Church in England. More, a devout Catholic, could not countenance such a move, and resigned his post. In 1535, he was put on trial for high treason. As a commoner, he was sentenced to be hanged, drawn and quartered, but the king commuted this to beheading. More's severed head was, as was customary at the time, exposed on a pike on London Bridge. In a daring act, his daughter rescued it before it was disposed of in the Thames.

3. ANNE BOLEYN (1536)

Anne became Henry's second wife in 1533. That year she gave birth – to a daughter, Elizabeth. In January 1536, Anne's second pregnancy ended in a miscarriage; the child had been a boy. Henry, by now in his mid-40s, was running out of time: he needed an heir, and, obviously, another wife. Trumped-up charges of adultery were quickly thrown against Anne: for a queen consort, adultery was treason, and treason was a capital offence. Five of her alleged lovers – including her own brother – were executed a week before she herself lost her head. The day after the beheading of Anne, once his heart's passion, Henry announced his engagement to wife number three, Jane Seymour.

4. THOMAS CROMWELL (1540)

Jane Seymour gave birth to a baby boy in October 1537. Henry at last had an heir, Prince Edward. Sadly the boy's mother died soon afterwards from birth complications. Henry immediately set about finding another wife: in the sixteenth century a child could easily die young, so it was standard dynastic practice to have two sons – one as backup, as it were. A marriage was arranged with Anne, daughter of the Duke of Cleves, a Protestant duchy in the Rhineland. Unfortunately, the allegedly beautiful Anne of Cleeves turned out, at least in Henry's eyes, to be 'a Flanders mare'. Repelled by her, he was unable to consummate the union and the marriage was annulled. Thomas Cromwell, a blacksmith's son who had risen to become Henry's principal advisor, had been in charge of the marriage arrangements, and so he became the scapegoat for Henry's displeasure. Cromwell, the most brilliant and hardworking of public servants, was subsequently beheaded as a traitor.

5. CATHERINE HOWARD (1542)

Catherine was Henry's fifth wife. He was almost 50, fat, and with painful ulcerous legs. She was a 19-year-old sexpot. Perhaps not surprisingly, she sought out the company of vigorous and attractive young men. Presented with the evidence of her multiple adulteries, Henry threatened to kill her with a sword himself. In the end, Catherine was beheaded in February 1542. Lady Rochford, Catherine's accomplice in the subterfuges, was also executed, and the heads of two of Catherine's lovers, Francis Dereham and Thomas Culpepper, decorated the pikes on London Bridge.

6. THE EARL OF SURREY (1547)

As Henry approached death, it became obvious that, as Prince Edward was still only 9 years old, a regent would be needed until the boy reached his majority. In 1546, therefore, various nobles started competing for the post of Protector of the Realm – an appointment that would make the winner the most powerful man in the kingdom. In January 1547, the earl – who had annoyed Henry by acting as though the job was already his – was brought out of the Tower of London and his head separated from his neck. His father, long one of Henry's most loyal subjects, was also executed.

Less than two weeks later, Henry VIII died.

EDWARD VI: FAMILY FEUDS AND PLOTS

'The Duke of Somerset had his head cut off upon Tower Hill between eight and nine o'clock in the morning.'

The diary of King Edward VI aged 13¾

A few days after the death of old King Henry, the council declared one man as the sole Protector of all the Realms and Dominions of the King's Majesty: Edward Seymour, the Duke of Somerset and Edward VI's uncle.

On the night of 16 January 1549, his brother, Thomas Seymour, stole towards Edward VI's bedchamber, armed with a pistol. He intended to kidnap the king and seize the Protectorate. It was a desperate, high-risk attempt at a *coup d'état*, and it failed because of a small dog.

As Thomas tried the lock, the boy-king's pet dog barked in warning. Thomas promptly shot the creature – and the report brought the guards running. Two months later, the Duke of Somerset signed his brother's death warrant:

EDWARD VI

Thomas Seymour, Lord High Admiral of England, was executed for treason on 20 March.

Edward Seymour was the next to fall, outmanoeuvred by the clever Earl of Warwick (and later the Duke of Northumberland) John Dudley, who gathered an army about him, captured the boy-king and threw Edward in the Tower. However, as Edward was popular, the earl could not have him executed. Around about this time Edward VI, now 14, started to show signs of ill-health: Dudley, recognising that the king might die young, set about securing absolute power for himself.

Firstly, the Duke of Somerset was accused of a ridiculous series of treasonable activities, including menacing the king. He was executed on Tower Hill.

Secondly, Dudley worked his charm on the king, who by 1552 was gravely ill with tuberculosis. After a vigorous propaganda campaign, Dudley finally persuaded the king to bar his two royal sisters, Mary and Elizabeth, from the succession, and instead specify in his will that the crown should pass to a distant claimant – Lady Jane Grey. Dudley had just had her married off to his own son, Guildford Dudley. Dudley now controlled all the pieces on the board: his main rival was dead; he was the Protector of the Realm in all but name; and the future queen was his daughter-in-law and puppet.

Edward VI died on 6 July 1553; he was 16. Dudley immediately launched his coup, and Lady Jane Grey was declared queen on 10 July. But what should have been a smooth transfer of power turned out to be a disaster. Both the royal princesses, Mary and Elizabeth, remained out of Dudley's clutches. Then Lady Jane Grey began to refuse to do what she was told, and the Dudleys and the Greys started to fall out. Eventually, Dudley was forced to head out on campaign to quell the growing unrest. With the principal hard man gone, the rest wavered, and then ran. On 18 July, the coup was over: Lady Jane Grey had been queen for just nine days. On 12 February 1554, she was beheaded on Tower Green.

Windsor Castle, where the king and Seymour were captured.
(LOC, LC-DIG-ppmsc-08598)

BLOODY MARY

'The burning question.'

Phrase first used by Edward Miall MP, nineteenth century

Bloody Mary I.

The dead dog came sailing through the window of the queen's presence chamber at Whitehall. As it landed, it could be seen that its ears had been cropped and its head shaved in a tonsure – to make it resemble a Catholic monk.

The cat was found in Friday Street, in the heart of London. It had been dressed in the vestments of a priest of Rome, and between its paws was a piece of bread, representing the sacramental host of the Catholic Mass. To emphasise the point, the cat had been hanged ...

The farce of Lady Jane Grey's nine-day reign had been followed by genuine national celebration when Mary, the daughter of Henry VIII and Katherine of Aragon, was crowned queen. Mary was deeply religious herself – she sometimes took Mass nine times a day – and had not noticed that, by the time she came to the throne in 1553, England had been getting progressively more Protestant for two decades.

Mary had been poorly served by life in her early years: she came to the throne almost middle-aged, never having known love or a husband. She started her reign by suppressing the Protestant rite of worship and making the Catholic Mass universally compulsory. This was followed by a marriage alliance with Catholic Spain, a move almost universally detested. When the first Spaniards arrived in London in January 1554, they were pelted with snowballs.

A short time later in Kent, 5,000 men rose in rebellion against the alliance with Spain – their war cry was, 'We are all Englishmen!' Led by Sir Thomas Wyatt, an effective leader and son of one of Henry VIII's courtiers, the rebels stormed London, only to be defeated by a larger force loyal to the Crown. Something like 120 of the captured rebels were executed, including Wyatt, who, under torture, implicated Mary's younger half-sister, the Protestant Lady Elizabeth, in the rebellion. Wyatt recanted this confession on the scaffold, and although Elizabeth was arrested and imprisoned in the Tower, in the end there was no strong evidence against her, and she was released.

Mary and Phillip II of Spain were married at Winchester Cathedral on 25 July 1554. In early 1555, the burning of Protestants started. A law dating back to 1401 allowed heretics to be burned alive – Henries IV and V knew this law very well. In total, 283 people were burned alive for heresy in four years, including Bishops Latimer and Ridley. Even those who recanted at the stake and swore to convert to Catholicism were not spared.

By 1558, having been queen for five years, Mary was ill, still childless after two false pregnancies, and despairing at a marriage that had gone nowhere.

AN
ABRIDGEMENT
OF THE BOOKE OF ACTS
AND MONVMENTES OF
THE CHVRCH:
Written by that Reuerend Father, Mai-
ſter Iohn Fox : and now abridged by Timothe Bright,
Doctour of Phiſicke, for ſuch as either through
want of leyſure, or abilitie, haue not the
vſe of ſo neceſſary an hiſtory.

All day long are we counted as ſheep for the ſlaughter. Pſal. 44.

How long Lord, holy and true? Apocal. Cap. 6, verſe 10.

Imprinted at London by I.Windet, at the aſſignment
of Maſter Tim.Bright, and are to be ſold at Pauls wharf,
at the ſigne of the Croſſe-keyes. 1589.
Cum gratia, & Priuilegio Regiæ Maieſtatis.

Contemporary title page from an abridgment of Foxe's *Book of Martyrs* showing the Pope slaughtering allegorical sheep whilst, in the background, two men burn.

When she died later that year she was universally sneered at as 'Spanish Mary'. In many ways Mary could be viewed as the most tragic of the Tudors – were it not for the lingering odour of burning human flesh.

MARY, QUEEN OF SCOTS

'Do not bring your Queen out too early.'

Francisco Bernardina Calogno, 'On the Game of Chess', written around 1500

Elizabeth I as Gloriana, the Virgin Queen.

Mary, Queen of Scots was singularly unfortunate in her three husbands. The first, Francis I of France, was initially a promising choice. Mary was brought up in the French court from the age of 5, and she and Francis married when she was 16 and he 15. Unfortunately, the teenage king died of an infection a year later; Mary was now, from the French point of view, redundant, and so she returned to Scotland in 1561.

Husband #2 was, not to put too fine a point on it, rubbish. Henry, Lord Darnley was an Anglo-Scottish aristocrat with more vices than virtues. In March 1566, Darnley and a group of conspirators murdered Mary's private secretary in front of her and held the now-pregnant queen hostage. He was later found smothered following the destruction of his home in an explosion.

Mary may or may not have had foreknowledge of the planned assassination. Almost certainly, however, one of Darnley's murderers was the Earl of Bothwell, who swiftly became Mary's third husband – after having kidnapped and possibly raped her. Mary and Bothwell were hardly a dream team, and the queen and king consort found themselves facing

Mary, Queen of Scots (LOC, LC-US262-121212)

there were many – the Catholic Duke of Norfolk planned to marry Mary and seize the throne, for example, while in 1571, a Catholic rebellion in the North of England used the symbol of Mary as its figurehead. The same year, a conspiracy was uncovered implicating Catholic Spain. More plots mounted over the years.

Mary believed that her coded secret letters, smuggled out in classic espionage fashion in the false stoppers of wine barrels, were secure. In fact, they were being read by Elizabeth's spymaster Sir Francis Walsingham, who had secreted a network of informants around what he regarded as the most serious domestic threat to Elizabeth's reign. In 1586, one of Mary's letters showed that she had authorised Elizabeth's assassination. She was arrested, tried for treason and eventually executed.

Seventeen years after Mary Queen of Scots got her head chopped off, Elizabeth I, one of England's greatest monarchs, passed away of old age. Her successor was not a Tudor, but a Stuart: James VI of Scotland, Mary Stuart's son.

a rebellion. Mary was forced to abdicate in favour of her 1-year-old son and imprisoned on a castle in the middle of a loch. She escaped, raised another army, was defeated, and so, in 1568, took the only route that seemed open to her – to flee to the England of Elizabeth I.

Mary seemed to believe that her cousin-queen would help her regain her throne. Instead, over the next eighteen years, she found herself a 'house guest' in various English castles, mostly chosen so that they were *A* nowhere near Scotland, *B* nowhere near London and *C* far from the sea, thus impeding rescue by conspirators. For conspirators and plots,

The signature and signet ring of Mary, Queen of Scots.

'BLOOD POURING FROM THE SCUPPERS'

'We are sailing against England in the confident hope of a miracle.'

Don Martín de Bertendona, one of the leaders of the Spanish Armada

The huge ship's thirty cannon were silenced, its upper decks a catastrophe of corpses and splintered timbers. As it heeled before the wind to once more plunge into a hell of gunfire and smoke, sailors in a nearby vessel saw an astonishing sight: blood pouring in gouts from the scuppers.

The ship was the *Ragazzona*, a mighty ocean-going carrack or cargo vessel converted for combat. At 1,294 tons, she was the largest ship in the Spanish Armada. Minutes earlier, she had been carrying eighty sailors and 233 soldiers. Many of them were now dead, victims of deadly cannon-shot inflicted by the English ships. Yet, despite the damage, the *Ragazzona* once more entered the fray, in defence of one of her sister ships. The musketeers who were still alive poured down fire from their positions in the rigging. The ship's captain, Don Martín de Bertendona, was not the kind of man to back down when the going got tough.

The incident took place during the Battle of Gravelines. For the past week, the English and Spanish fleets had fought a series of inconclusive running battles up the length of the south coast of England, as the Armada headed to its rendezvous with an invasion force of thousands of battle-hardened troops waiting to cross the Channel from the Spanish Netherlands (modern-day Belgium). Now, in the seas between Calais and Dunkirk, the final engagement took place. The night before, the English had sent unmanned fireships to drift into the massed ranks of the enemy warships. Although none of the floating incendiaries hit a target, their presence had caused many Spanish captains to panic and cut their anchors as they scrambled to remove themselves from the deadly flames. Up to this point, the Armada had sailed in a formidable crescent-shaped formation, a brilliant naval innovation that the men of England had never seen before – and which had proved impossible for the English fleet to attack effectively. Now, with the confusion caused by the fireships dispersing the formation, Elizabeth's sea-dogs – Sir Francis Drake, Martin Frobisher, Sir John Hawkins and others – mounted what they hoped would be the decisive attack

One of the legendary moments in the Armada saga – the Spanish have been sighted,
the warning beacons lit, and Sir Francis Drake calmly continues playing bowls.

Despite their superb seamanship, militarily, the Spanish were from a previous age. The major Spanish ships were basically floating castles. Their preferred tactic was to fire their heavy guns once, then close in and either ram the enemy ship or come alongside – and then send over massed boarding parties. Once their superior numbers had told in the melee, they would have captured a valuable ship, and perhaps officers who could be

All this was essentially medieval thinking. The English, however, were on the cutting edge of maritime military technology. Instead of fighting a land war at sea, they were fighting a sea war at sea. In contrast to the lumbering giants of the Spanish, the English ships were nippier, more manoeuvrable, and armed with lighter cannon that could be reloaded many times faster than the unwieldy Spanish guns, which were more suited for bombarding a castle

In addition, boarding parties were completely out of the picture: the new English tactic was to keep just out of boarding range and batter the enemy vessels with short-range cannon until the Spanish galleons either sank or were rendered useless. The Spanish kept wanting to close in and board, and the English kept denying them that intention. Just one overenthusiastic English sailor grabbed a rope to swing aboard a Spanish ship – and he was instantly cut down.

A vivid if entirely inaccurate imagining
of the Battle of Gravelines.

After almost nine hours of cannonading – slow an irregular on the Spanish side, fast and metronomic o the English side – five major Spanish ships had been sunk or taken. The carnage was appalling. Probabl some 600 Spanish sailors, soldiers and noblemen were dead, many cut in half by huge flying wooden shards, while hundreds of others were wounded. A about four in the afternoon, the English were driving the Spanish closer and closer to the deadly shoals o the European coastline when the weather suddenly changed, a fierce squall blinding every lookout and reducing visibility to a few yards. The English captain frantically manoeuvred, desperate not to collide with other friendly vessels. The squall saved the Spanish when it cleared, they had avoided the shoals an sandbanks and were heading north. Despite th battering, the majority of the Armada was still intac The English, however, failed to follow up on thei advantage, and the still formidable Spanish leviathan headed north into open waters.

To the Victorians and Edwardians,
Sir Francis Drake was the greatest of heroes

The Armada, however, was in no fit state to continue fighting. It made an immense sweep around the north of Scotland and the west coast of Ireland, heading back to Spain. Unfortunately, 1588 was the year of one of the worst storms of the century. Sixty-one ships were lost. Perhaps some 20,000 men died of drowning, exposure, starvation, thirst, disease, or, if they made it ashore, by being murdered by the local Irish, or by English militias. For all its smoke and noise, the Battle of Gravelines had been a relatively minor affair: the Armada's real defeat came at the hands of the weather gods.

The English had lost no ships and only about 100 men. And, as sure as winter follows summer, after the victory came the mismanagement. Unsure whether the Armada was going to return, under-provisioned English ships were kept at sea – and perhaps more than 6,000 men died of disease, mostly typhus, the sailor's most-feared enemy. And when the survivors returned home, often they did so without the wages due to them. Once the fighting was over, the men who did the fighting were forgotten and badly treated: a grim story repeated into our days.

Despite this abysmal treatment, and despite the fact that the invasion had been avoided by a hair's breadth, the defeat of the Spanish Armada immediately entered national mythology. It bolstered Elizabeth's rule and created a legend that embroidered English self-regard for centuries to come.

The sea *v.* the Spanish Armada.

The *Ragazzona*, by the way, made it back to Spain, a tribute to the extraordinary seamanship of her captain Bertendona and his skeleton crew. In fact, over half of the Armada eventually limped home, and the Spanish immediately put into effect the lessons they had learned from the defeat. The next time the two nations clashed at sea, the Spanish had the upper hand: and, despite English propaganda, Spain continued to rule the high seas for years to come.

KEEPING UP WITH THE JAMESES

'Let us sit upon the ground, and tell sad stories of the death of kings.'

Shakespeare, Richard II

The Royal House of Stuart first gained the throne of Scotland in 1371. For more than two centuries, the family ruled a turbulent kingdom where the status of the monarchy was often held in low esteem, where Scots-speaking Lowlanders of the south distrusted the Gaelic-speaking Highlanders of the North, where clan warfare was endemic, and where nobles often thought themselves mightier than their kings. Not that different from England, then, but perhaps with worse weather.

The first of the line, Robert II, was 54 when he gained the throne and his successor, Robert III, had to wait until he was 53 to become king. At these ages, both men were old by medieval standards, and neither had a happy reign. Robert III in particular, disabled by a horse's kick and conspired against by his relatives, left a deathbed statement whose self-pity and pain echoes down the centuries: 'Bury me in a midden and write, "Here lies the worst of kings and the most wretched of men."'

After Robert III, the dynasty had an unbroken line of six Jameses, the first five of whom all came to sticky ends:

JAMES I OF SCOTLAND (DIED 1437)

A group of armed nobles burst into the king's apartments at the Dominican Friary in Perth, injured the queen, and pursued James, who tried to escape through a latrine drain – which he himself had unfortunately had blocked up because he kept losing his tennis balls down it. Somewhat corpulent, James got stuck and was run through. The conspirators were later caught and subjected to tortures more extreme than even the usual medieval levels of savagery.

JAMES II OF SCOTLAND (DIED 1460)

A fan of the new technology of artillery, James was supervising the bombardment of the English-held Roxburgh Castle in the Scottish Borders when a large Flanders cannon known as 'the Lion' misfired and exploded. James was standing right next to the cannon and his leg was smashed in two. He died quickly, either from shock or loss of blood.

JAMES III OF SCOTLAND (DIED 1488)

Another king hemmed in by his nobles (who in this case included his own brothers), James' rather miserable final years culminated in defeat and death at the Battle of Sauchieburn near Stirling, where the opposing army was led, at least nominally, by his own teenage son. Sited only a couple of miles from the lustily celebrated Battle of Bannockburn, Sauchieburn is one of the great forgotten battles of Scottish history, probably because its sordid domestic context is neither inspirational nor useful for knee-jerk English-bashing.

JAMES IV OF SCOTLAND (DIED 1513)

This James is the most impressive of the lot – a true king who actually ruled his kingdom, kept the nobles in check, built up the navy, inspired the arts, and did what no other Scottish monarch had ever been able to achieve – bring the independent-minded Lords of the Isles to heel, thus extending the power of his kingdom into the hitherto-ungovernable Hebrides on the west coast. In fact, intellectual, cultured and vigorous James IV would stand in the same category of Renaissance princes as Henry VIII – were it not for the slight miscalculation of losing one of the greatest battles of the age, a battle he need not have fought. Ever since 1295, France and Scotland had operated on the policy of 'my enemy's enemy is my friend' – because both found England somewhat inconvenient. In 1513, Henry VIII invaded France. Called to assist his French ally under the terms of the 'Auld Alliance', James reluctantly invaded England with an

A Victorian view of the slaughter at Flodden Field.

enormous army – something like 40,000 men, perhaps more. On 9 September, this huge force confronted an English army of 26,000 at Flodden Field near Coldstream in Northumberland – and was utterly defeated. Perhaps 10,000 Scots died, including twelve earls, fourteen lords, and at least one member from each of the country's leading families: plus the king himself, fighting to the end until he was cut down. The impact on the Scottish political and economic situation was catastrophic, and the nation took the best part of a generation to recover.

JAMES V OF SCOTLAND (DIED 1542)

Coming to the throne aged just 1 meant that this James grew up in the typical snakepit of competing nobles and relatives, which wasn't going to make for a strong kingship. In 1542, James offended Henry VIII, who responded with an invasion. On 24 November, around 18,000 Scots confronted 3,000 English troops at Solway Moss, north of Carlisle. It was another disaster for the Scots, who lost perhaps twenty men to the sword, but hundreds to the waters of the River Esk. James had not been present at the battle but, already sick, he retired in humiliation to Falkland Palace, where his entire physical and mental well being seems to have collapsed; he died having heard that he was the father of a newborn daughter, and that the male line of the Stuarts was, as he thought, at an end.

JAMES VI OF SCOTLAND AND I OF ENGLAND (DIED 1625)

The end, however, had not come. This James was the son of that daughter, Mary, Queen of Scots, and James V's grandson. With him the game changed forever – for in 1603 he succeeded to the throne of England: the England with colonies in the New World, the England with a grand navy, the England with a grand and glittering court, the England of greater wealth and greater power than his northern kingdom could muster. Perhaps not surprisingly, James went back to Scotland only once. When he died of illness in 1625 he had been King of Scotland for almost fifty-eight years, an astonishing achievement given the short lifespan of many of his predecessors.

GUNPOWDER, TREASON AND PLOT

'... that most horrid and hellish conspiracy ...'

Part title of a book published in 1662

The Gunpowder Plot of 1605 was something entirely new: not just an attempt to assassinate the king, but a device designed to, at one stroke, kill several members of the Royal Family, all the Members of Parliament, all the peers of the realm, all the law lords, all the bishops, and, as collateral damage, dozens of servants, employees and guards and hundreds of ordinary Londoners who had assembled to watch the annual opening of Parliament. It was the first use of mass terrorism in British history.

Contemporary portraits of the plotters, showing (from left to right)
Thomas Bates, Robert Winter, the Wright brothers, Thomas Percy, Guy Fawkes, Sir Robert Catesby and Thomas Winter.

The source of the plot was the unhealed scab of English life and law: what to do about Catholicism. Many prominent families, especially in the North, were still adherents of Rome. When Elizabeth's legal restrictions against English Catholics were not lifted by the new king, a group of militants decided that only assassination would do the job. With Parliament House and Westminster Abbey a smoking ruin, and the entire apparatus of government annihilated, they planned to seize Princess Elizabeth, James' eldest daughter, and make her their puppet queen.

The conspirators rented the building next to Parliament House and dug a tunnel heading towards the cellar below Parliament. Sometime later they discovered that the cellar itself could simply be rented, which made their job of storing the barrels of gunpowder that much easier. In total, thirty-six barrels were hidden beneath Parliament.

The New Houses of Parliament, incorporating Westminster Palace, which narrowly avoided being blown to pieces in this era. Guy Fawkes was tried inside. (LOC, LC-DIG-ppmsc-08560)

Unfortunately, one of the conspirators sent a relative a letter warning him not to attend the opening. In the early hours of 5 November the cellar was searched, the cache of explosives discovered, and a man who later revealed his name as Guy Fawkes was arrested. As the scale of the planned atrocity became clear, the whole of London was placed 'under arms' and that evening church bells rang out and many bonfires were lit. The second locus was a house called Holbeach in Staffordshire, the final destination of the fleeing plotters, who had ridden out of London on hearing the news of the discovery and then been chased through Warwickshire and Worcestershire. Holbeach was the scene of a desperate last stand. According to the official account, two and a half

Letter which revealed the Gunpowder Plot.

Print from twenty years after the Gunpowder Plot showing the grace of God foiling the Devil (pictured in the centre with the Pope and various churchmen) and his Catholic wiles: the Armada on the left and the Guy Fawkes carrying in the explosives on the right. (LOC, LC-USZ62-86540)

pounds of gunpowder drying in front of the fire was touched by a burning coal and exploded, injuring several of the men and blowing up the roof of the house. A bag containing a further sixteen pounds of gunpowder was blown into the courtyard, but failed to explode – had it done so, the besieged party would have just been a collection of body parts. As it was, the first explosion provided just the opportunity the assailants needed. During the frontal assault four of the plotters were killed, including the two principal conspirators, Thomas Percy and Sir Robert Catesby, reportedly shot by the same bullet.

Fawkes was a professional soldier who had fought for the Catholic cause in the Netherlands. He withstood the torture of the rack for some time before naming his co-conspirators and revealing details of the preparations. Being the only one caught at the scene of the crime, he became known as 'the devil in the vault' and it was his infamy that meant that, out of all the plotters, he is the one who is still remembered to this day. Despite what many people think, Fawkes was not burned at the stake or on a bonfire, but, along with eight other conspirators, hanged on the 30 and 31 of January 1606, their bodies thereafter being divided into quarters, the traditional punishment for traitors. The bonfires of Bonfire Night actually commemorate those warning fires lit on 5 November 1605.

Torture on the rack in action.

TO KILL A KING: THE EXECUTION OF CHARLES I

'A bloody deed! Almost as bad, good mother, as kill a king.'

Shakespeare, *Hamlet*

6.30 a.m. The king woke before dawn, disturbed by his servant's groaning from a nightmare. He dressed in his best clothes, adding a second shirt to combat the icy cold. He did not want to shiver, lest his shivering be interpreted as fear.

10.00 a.m. A knock at the door. 'Come, let us go,' said the king. From St James's Palace he crossed St James's Park to the sound of slow, regular drumming.

10.30 a.m. The king waited in his old bedroom in Whitehall Palace, its former magnificence now stripped bare. He ate a loaf of bread and drank some claret. Then he prayed.

1642. For the first time in English history, a king enters the House of Commons with an armed band and attempts to arrest some of the Members of Parliament. Parliament and the king are now irreconcilable. Eight months later, Charles raises his standard at Nottingham: the English Civil War has begun.

2.00 p.m. Another knock at the door. The king was led through the Banqueting Hall at Whitehall and stepped out through a first-floor window directly onto the black-draped scaffold.

1642–48. An endless series of battles: Powick Bridge, Edgehill, Newbury, Cropredy Bridge, Marston Moor, Montgomery, Naseby, Philiphaugh, St Fagans ... Royalists (popularly called 'Cavaliers') wage war against Parliamentarians ('Roundheads'). Oliver Cromwell establishes a professional Parliamentarian army, the New Model Army. Scottish Covenanter forces fight on the side of the Parliamentarians in England. Royalists struggle against Covenanters in Scotland. Irish troops invade Scotland. Parliamentarians go on the attack in Ireland. Gloucester, Oxford, Bristol, York, Chester, Colchester, Pembroke and dozens of other places are besieged. Religious, political and military factions make bids for power. Rebellions in support of various groups break out in Kent, Essex and Wales. Commanders change sides. Troops mutiny. Riots erupt in Canterbury, London and Norwich. Families are divided by their loyalties. The country is traumatised.

Charles R

King Charles I, his seal, and his signature.

King Charles' Tower in Chester, from which the king reputedly watched the Battle of Rowton Heath.

2.08 p.m. 'Take care they do not put me in pain,' said the king, eying the axe. Beheading was supposedly a clean, quick death, but there had been many occasions where it had taken two, three or even more strokes for the axe to do its job.

1646. Charles surrenders to the Scots besieging Newark. The following year he is handed over to the English Parliament (in exchange for £100,000), only to escape in November and go on the run.

2.10 p.m. The king tucked his long hair under his satin nightcap, ensuring that his neck was free.

1647–48. Charles signs a secret treaty with the Scots, whose Presbyterianism he formerly tried to suppress. Despite his Roman Catholic wife, Charles agrees that when he regains the throne he will make England a Presbyterian nation. In exchange, the Scots invade England.

2.12 p.m. The king gave his Garter insignia to his chaplain William Juxon, uttering the enigmatic word 'remember'.

1648. The Royalists are defeated for the final time. Negotiations are opened between king and Parliament, but Oliver Cromwell's hard-line anti-Charles party removes its opponents from Parliament. There will be no further diplomacy.

Oliver Cromwell
and his signature.

2.16 p.m. The king prayed a little.

1649. Charles is publicly put on trial for high treason.

2.20 p.m. The executioner's block was very low, and the king was a tall man. He was forced to lie on the floor to place his neck in the correct position.

27 January 1649. The court gives its verdict: 'Charles Stuart as a tyrant, traitor, murderer and public enemy to the good people of this nation, shall be put to death by the severing of his head from his body.'

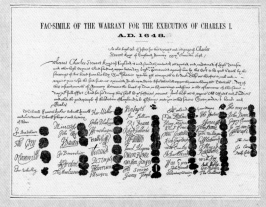

Death warrant for Charles I.

2.21 p.m. The axe severed the king's head from his neck in one single sweep. Charles I, King of England, Scotland and Ireland, was dead. For the first and only time in British history, a reigning monarch had been executed by his own people.

The year 1649 marked a sea change in British history. It wasn't just that a king had been put on trial and executed for treason: it was that the entire monarchy itself had been abolished. England (including Wales) was declared a republic, a nation where, for the first time, kings and queens had no place. As is often the way of revolutions, these immense events also unleashed a wave of new thinking about how society should work. Radical fringe groups – such as the Levellers and the Diggers and many others – challenged the social order. Religious sects flourished. The flavour of the period can be characterised by the title of a famous contemporary pamphlet: 'The World Turned Upside Down'.

What is usually called the English Civil War was in fact three separate wars (1642–46, 1648–49 and 1649–51) that splattered a generation's blood across England, Wales, Scotland and Ireland. Taking into account the handmaidens of war – famine, disease and untreated combat-related infection – perhaps 190,000 people died in England and Wales, while the death figure for Scotland was around 60,000. Ireland's principal suffering took place in 1649–51, during which an astonishing 600,000 may have perished – perhaps 40 per cent of the total population.

As for Charles, many people saw him as a martyr to his conscience. Others have been less kind. He was pig-headed, duplicitous, shifty and rather weak, making him a prime candidate for one of the more lauded titles in British history: worst king ever.

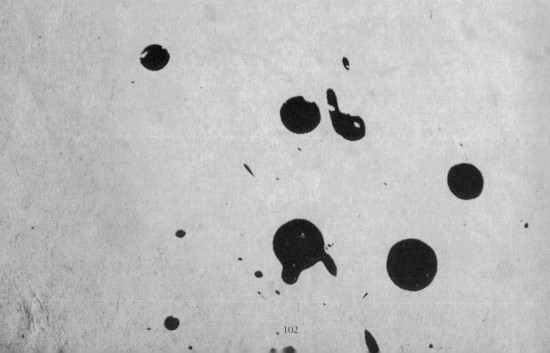

THE GREATEST SEA BATTLE OF THE AGE

'The war is begun: God give a good end to it.'

Samuel Pepys, Diary, 1665

The Battle of Lowestoft, fought off the east coast of England on 13 June 1665, was not only a resounding victory for the Royal Navy, but the greatest sea battle of the age to boot.

The backdrop, as ever, was money. Or, rather, wealth. Spain had grown fat on the goods imported from its great empire in the Americas. After a time, two upstart nations – England and the Netherlands – challenged Spanish naval supremacy in the Atlantic. Sparks started to fly between the two aggressive, ambitious North Sea neighbours. The conflict waxed and waned for years. Finally, duplicitous Albion pulled off a textbook 'dirty tricks' ruse: English ships supposedly under private ownership attacked and took Dutch colonies in both Africa and the New World (one of the American places they acquired was known as

The pier at Lowestoft.
Some 40 miles out to sea, the greatest
sea battle of the age was waged.
(LOC, LC-DIG-ppmsc-08617)

New Amsterdam – now a place of little importance called, I believe, New York, or something like that). In reality, the 'shareholders' in the private ventures were King Charles II, other members of the Royal Family, and the Royal Navy's most senior admirals, all of whom profited mightily from the prizes taken. Provoked beyond endurance, the Dutch declared war – which is exactly what the English had wanted. To its powerful European peers, England portrayed itself as the innocent, aggrieved victim of an unjustified war.

The scale of the two fleets at the resulting battle was astonishing. The Dutch fleet consisted of 103 armed ships, plus thirty fireships and dispatch boats, while the English fielded no less than 109 men-of-war and twenty-eight fireships, making a total of 270 vessels for both sides. (In comparison, the two opposing fleets at Trafalgar had seventy-four ships between them, although admittedly the ships in 1805 were much larger.) In terms of manpower, the Dutch had 21,631 men against 21,006 English sailors, while their ships were

Two years after the Battle of Lowestoft, the Dutch sailed into the heart of Kent and destroyed several Royal Navy ships in the dockyard at Chatham.

carrying 4,869 guns versus the English armoury of 4,192 (usually heavier and longer-range) cannon. When the English fleet lined up in battle order, it was no less than 5 miles in length.

Manoeuvring and co-ordinating the huge fleets proved to be an insurmountable problem for both sides, especially as the wind kept changing direction. After a first ineffective pass between the two fleets, when large amounts of cannonballs and grapeshot were fired to relatively little effect, squadron discipline seems to have broken down on both sides. A melee ensued. Thoughts of personal glory overcame battle orders, and individual leaders sought out their opposite numbers in what were effectively ship-to-ship duels. The Earl of Sandwich, for example, commanding the 86-gun *Royal Prince*, deliberately engaged the Dutch commander-in-chief Jacob van Wassenaer on his flagship, the 76-gun *Eendracht*. Meanwhile, on the 78-gun *Royal Charles*, the Lord High Admiral the Duke of York (later King James II) was drenched in blood as chain shot from the *Oranje* decapitated several of his courtiers who had been standing timidly beside him on the quarterdeck. The brutal engagement brought in several other capital ships on both sides before it was brought to an abrupt end when the mighty *Eendracht* took a hit in her powder magazine and exploded in a vast sheet of flame that killed 404 out of her crew of 409. The explosion could be heard in the Dutch capital, The Hague, some 60 miles away.

At this point, a major flaw in the Dutch navy proved fatal. The Netherlands was strictly the United Provinces, a federation of seven provinces,

each of which was jealous and suspicious of the others. As a result, the Dutch fleet may have had one commander-in-chief, but it had numerous seconds-in-command, each one from a different province. With van Wassenaer dead, no less than three admirals hoisted the flag of overall command, causing immense confusion as captains struggled to know which one to follow.

Amidst the chaos, Dutch warships collided with each other – and became the victim of the English fireships. The fireships were justifiably feared – they were effectively tactical floating bombs. At the time, it was relatively rare for a man-of-war to be sunk by cannon fire alone, but being wooden, they were vulnerable to fire. Fireships were manned by small crews who sailed their vessels directly at the enemy. At the last minute the crew set off an incendiary mixture in the hold and then abandoned ship in a small rowing boat – but not before jamming the rudder of their suicide vessel. If the wind continued in the same direction, the burning hulk would hit or graze the enemy man-of-war, and the flames would do the rest.

As darkness fell, the Dutch were in full retreat, having lost thirty ships, three admirals and at least 5,000 men. The English had suffered the loss of only two ships and around 800 men; despite their clear numerical superiority, however, their fleet failed to pursue the Dutch, and thus the English lost out on the chance to end the war once and for all. The general consensus is that the future James II, or his entourage, not being exactly military men, had slowed the chase because they had had enough bloodshed for one day.

AD 1666

LONDON'S BURNING!

'A woman might p*ss it out.'

Sir Thomas Bludworth, Lord Mayor, on first seeing what would become the Great Fire

First came the plague. It wasn't the Black Death, but the bacillus responsible was nevertheless a keen harvester of humans: almost 100,000 Londoners died in 1665. Bodies were left on the streets to be collected by the death carts and taken to the mass plague pits. It was fully expected that the plague would return to the city in the warmer months of the following year, but in the end only 1,800 plague deaths were recorded for London in 1666 – although the provinces suffered appallingly: Cambridge lost a quarter of its population, while Colchester and Braintree in Essex saw mortality rates of more than 40 per cent.

The Great Fire of London.

Then came the heatwave and the drought. Both 1665 and 1666 were unusually dry, with the summer of 1666 being the hottest for years. In the south-east, rivers were low and many streams and lakes disappeared. The moment for disaster had come.

At about one o'clock on the morning of Sunday, 2 September 1666, a small fire broke out on the ground floor of a house in Pudding Lane, the property of Thomas Farriner, a baker of ship's biscuits for the navy. By the time the blaze was discovered the stairs were already impassable, so the family escaped through an upstairs window and crawled along a gutter. The maidservant, however, refused to make the hazardous rooftop journey across to the neighbour's house, and remained behind, thereby becoming the fire's first victim. By three in the morning, several of the adjacent houses were ablaze. The Lord Mayor refused to allow the demolition of nearby buildings to create a firebreak, as practice had shown that the firefighters would later be sued by the owners of the houses or businesses concerned. It was at this point that His Worship made the unfortunate remark quoted above.

That Sunday morning, it was blowing a gale. And Pudding Lane was at the heart of a densely packed concentration of lanes and alleys in the City of London, where the houses were made of wood and many of the tradesmen dealt in shipping products such as pitch, flax, tar, hemp and timber – all of which were of course combustible.

London, and indeed seventeenth-century England, was no stranger to fire. In 1630, fifty houses burned down in Southwark on the south bank of the Thames, while three years later, eighty houses on the north bank, along with many buildings on the densely populated London Bridge, were lost to fire. In 1650, seven barrels of gunpowder exploded on the premises of a ship's chandler, taking out more than forty houses and killing sixty-seven people. Outside the metropolis, 224 houses burned down at Marlborough (Wiltshire) in 1653, while Southwold (Suffolk) and Newport (Shropshire) lost 238 and 156 houses respectively in 1659 and 1665. To counteract this ever-present danger, by 1666 London had made the first steps towards fire control, with buckets available in church halls, and early fire engines on hand. Unfortunately, co-ordinated action was far in the future (indeed, it was not until 1824 that James Braidwood, Master of Fire Engines at Edinburgh, created a clear chain of command during a fire emergency – he later founded the London Fire Brigade). So as the 1666 conflagration advanced, firefighters suddenly found their hoses were dry, because the pipes had been cut further up the line by people who wanted the water exclusively for their part of the fire.

Another of London's 'Great Fires': this is London Bridge being destroyed in 1758.

The strong winds were the fire's best friend. Burning debris was carried far from the front line of the flames, setting up auxiliary fires that then joined with the major blaze. By Sunday evening, the Lord Mayor's men were desperately pulling down buildings, but it was far too late for firebreaks, and the materials left behind after the demolition were proving equally combustible. The fire was by now eating up about 100 houses an hour. By Monday morning, the streets and riverside were a chaos of people trying to flee with their belongings, and the hire-price of carts and light boats leapt several hundred per cent. Some shady entrepreneurs posing as porters were paid to remove furniture and other goods, and then skedaddled with the lot. In a typical street you

The monument which marks the place the Great Fire at last came to a stop.

might see some men fighting a blaze, a terrified family fleeing with whatever they could carry, and a gang engaged in wholesale looting. Rumours swept the city that the fire was no accident but a series of organised arson attacks, and foreigners of all kinds were attacked, some seriously, on such evidence as 'possession of incendiary devices' (actually tennis balls) and 'throwing a fireball' (in reality a piece of bread).

On Wednesday, the wind dropped. The numerous fires could now be tackled more effectively and most had been extinguished by early Thursday morning. For Londoners, many of whom had barely slept for four days, the noise, the smoke and the intensely hot air combined to give the impression that they had lived through some kind of apocalypse.

And indeed they had. Although the direct death toll was very low – just six, although many more perished in the months to come from the after-effects – the destruction was immense. The centre of one of the most densely populated cities in the world was now a vast open space where the only landmark was the occasional shell of a stone-built church. Some 85 per cent of the area of the City of London within the city walls had been gutted. St Paul's Cathedral was a smoking ruin, and the flames had only been turned back at the very gates of the Tower of London. At least 13,000 houses were destroyed, and between 65,000 and 80,000 Londoners were made homeless. The Great Fire of 1666 was London's single worst disaster in its history.

AD 1679

SCOTLAND INVENTS THE CONCENTRATION CAMP

'We have made a covenant with death, and with hell are we at agreement.'

Isaiah 28:15

In 1637, England and Scotland were entirely separate nations, but they shared the same Stuart king, Charles I. However, their religious histories were very different – the ultra-violent Scottish Reformation of 1560 had also been accompanied by a devastating civil war and the tug-of-war around the Catholic Mary, Queen of Scots – so when Charles tried to impose bishops on Scotland, large numbers of Presbyterians signed a National Covenant defending their religion, and the Covenanting Wars were born.

Signing the Covenant was to defy the will of the king: in other words, treason. The Covenanting Armies of these years were characterised by an extreme degree of religious fanaticism, making them highly motivated but often not particularly well led: generals were sometimes appointed not so much on their military abilities, but on their degree of religious fervour. And they fought on both sides: in 1650 an ill-judged invasion of England in support of Charles II saw Scotland occupied by Cromwell's Commonwealth Army for a decade.

The full horror of persecution, however, came after the Restoration. The Covenanters were now

vermin, to be hunted down wherever they congregated. Many were executed without trial after surrendering, while the scaffolds of Edinburgh and other cities groaned with mass hangings. Women were tied to stakes below the high-water level and forced to watch as the tide advanced to drown them. Severed heads adorned the city gates of Edinburgh, while the quartered bodies of rebels were nailed above the entrances to provincial cities. Perhaps 18,000 died during the Killing Times between 1661 and 1680, martyrs to their rigid faith.

It is usually stated that the British Army invented the concentration camp during the Boer War. Not so. Concentrating large numbers of captured enemies in one space under grim circumstances was actually the brainchild of the good citizens of Edinburgh. In 1679, the Covenanters were defeated at the Battle of Bothwell Bridge near Glasgow. Around 1,200 prisoners were force-marched to Edinburgh and imprisoned in a walled and gated open space within Greyfriars graveyard. This location had symbolic as well as practical value, as it was at Greyfriars that the

National Covenant had been circulated in 1638, with some of the more fanatical signatories dipping the quill into their own blood. Forty years on, it was to be the scene of an appalling atrocity.

The enclosure was open to all the joys of the Scottish autumn and winter, in a city noted for its cold and damp climate. Lacking shelter and blankets, and grudgingly given the barest minimum of bread and water, the Covenanters succumbed to disease, exposure and starvation. Hundreds died. Some, at the very end of their resources, signed an oath of allegiance to the king and were released. Others were hanged, while a very small number managed to escape.

The entrance to the open space where the Covenanters were imprisoned, Greyfriars, Edinburgh.

While the Established Church in England and Wales remains Anglican, to this day the Church of Scotland is Presbyterian – a direct result of the Covenanter last stand at Dunkeld.

By November 1679, after five months' open-air incarceration, 257 men remained, many of them walking skeletons. Their faith held firm, however, so the obvious solution was near-slavery in the New World, a common fate for troublesome and marginal individuals in seventeenth-century Scotland. They were shackled below decks in a ship destined for the American colonies – but the storm-bound vessel sank off the Orkney Islands, and all but forty-eight of the Covenanters were drowned.

In a way, the Covenanters were vindicated. In 1689, a tiny Covenanter force held a much larger Jacobite army at bay at the Battle of Dunkeld, their religious fervour and self-belief the key winning element in what was widely otherwise seen as a suicide mission. With Protestant William and Mary on the throne they were heroes, part of the frontline fight against the Jacobite rebels of James VII.

THE SIEGE OF DERRY

'No Surrender!'

Contemporary Derry graffiti

This is a tale of war, incompetence, prejudice, dog flesh and a little boy's bottom.

From Elizabeth I's time onwards, English monarchs had claimed all of Ireland as a separate kingdom. In the early seventeenth century, James I of England decided that, like America, Ireland had to turn a profit. In the north-west of the country, the old medieval remains of Derry were demolished and an entirely new town was built by stonemasons and carpenters brought over from London. Somewhat reluctantly, the merchants of London were persuaded to invest in the commercial opportunities presented

Derry (LOC, LC-DIG-ppmsc-09914)

by this new walled town and its fine Atlantic-facing port on the River Foyle. Protestants of all walks of life were imported from England and Scotland, and by the 1620s Derry was an established plantation, a walled and defended Protestant trading colony sitting in the midst of a largely Catholic hinterland.

In 1685 Charles II's brother, James II, came to the throne of the three kingdoms. James was a devout Catholic, and soon both the civil and military administrators in Ireland were no longer Protestant, but Catholic. At the end of 1688, the Protestant garrison was controversially withdrawn from Derry and the remaining citizens feared they were going to be massacred. As the replacement force of Catholic troops approached, a group of young men closed the city gates and refused them admission. This was an extraordinary event – denying them entry was tantamount to rebellion and treason. But these were not ordinary times – for England was in crisis.

Invited by the English Establishment who were dismayed by James' pro-Catholic policies, William of Orange (ruler of the Netherlands and the husband of James' Protestant daughter Mary) had landed in Devon with an enormous fleet of 463 ships and 15,000 battle-hardened soldiers. A month later, following just one minor skirmish, all James' military resistance had ignominiously collapsed, and he had fled the country for France. The 'Glorious Revolution', as it came to be known, made William and Mary joint Protestant monarchs.

In 1690 James landed in Ireland and, with an Irish, English and French Catholic army, tried to regain his

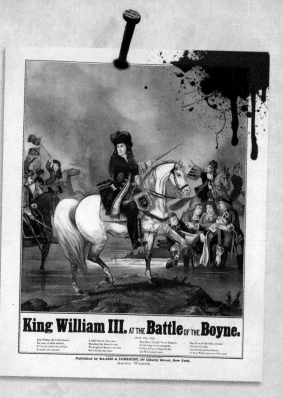

throne – with both James and William claiming to be the legitimate monarch, it was known as 'the Year of Two Kings'. In Derry, a new Protestant garrison had set up shop, and now thousands of Protestants from all over Ulster gathered within its protective walls. In April, James approached the city, seeking its submission to his royal authority. Instead, some of the defenders fired at the king, killing some of his party. That was shock number one. James then sat miserably on his horse all day in the pouring rain, waiting in vain for the city to capitulate. Shock two was the response: 'No Surrender.' Derry had struck a terrible blow to his prestige.

James ordered the city to be besieged. In truth, the siege was more of a blockade, as the Jacobites – as James' troops were known – did not have enough manpower or resources to overcome the defences. Despite a few vicious direct attacks, the operation largely came down to two actions: preventing any supplies from getting in by blockading the roads and building a barrage boom across the river; and firing hundreds of mortar bombs onto the town. Within the walls, people died either from the bombing or from starvation and disease: the total number of fatalities was in the many thousands. One of the residents,

George Walker, recorded a famous 'siege price list': both a quart of horse blood and a rat cost 1s, a dog's head 2s and sixpence, and a quarter of a dog ('fattened by eating the bodies of the slain Irish') went for 5½s. Water was scarce and contaminated. Outside the walls, things were hardly better: the Jacobites were poorly supplied with food and equipment and were completely unprepared for the appalling weather. Thousands died of cold and disease, while many others – wounded in the clashes – frequently succumbed to their injuries for lack of medical care. Morale plunged and many deserted.

In June, a small English relief fleet arrived but could not get past the river boom. At the end of July, however, a concerted effort smashed its way through. Although the Jacobites maintained the mortar bombardment for another three days, it was obvious that the siege was over, and they withdrew, having suffered grievous losses. The Siege of Derry had lasted for 108 bloody days.

Communications between the city and the English ships, by the way, were initially established via the means of a small boy who slipped through the enemy lines – with messages sewn into a suppository inserted into his bottom. The name of this colonic messenger has not been recorded, but surely his heroic efforts need to be commemorated in some suitable way.

James II of England, VII of Scotland, and
King of Ireland: not one of our better kings.

JACOBITE REBELLIONS

'My Bonnie Lies Over the Ocean.'

Traditional Scottish folk song

The earth-shattering events of the Glorious Revolution of 1689 had consequences that played out for decades to come, not least in the slightly grotesque family saga of the Stuarts.

The Stuarts had been kings of Scotland from 1371 and, barring the slight issue of Cromwell's republic, of England since 1603. Not surprisingly, they were loath to let go of several hundred years of ruling by divine right. After James II's humiliation at the Siege of Derry in 1689 and his subsequent catastrophic defeat by the Williamite forces at the Battle of the Boyne, Catholic James had fled to Catholic France. For more than fifty years, France plotted and pushed several generations of Stuarts into invading their homeland.

Glen Shiel, site of the almost-forgotten Jacobite invasion of the west of Scotland in 1719.

The year 1689 had seen more than just fighting in Ireland: in Scotland, a Jacobite force led by the brilliant Viscount Claverhouse had won a major victory at the Battle of Killiecrankie in Highland Perthshire, but Claverhouse's death at the very moment of his triumph, followed by a check at the Battle of Dunkeld, had seen the rebellion fizzle out, although the mopping up continued into the following year. Jacobite ambitions thereafter concentrated on Scotland and the North of England, both of which had significant Catholic populations, while many Scots, especially in the Highlands, retained an attachment to the House of Stuart. So it was that in 1715 a rebellion was raised in Scotland and the North on behalf of James II's son, Prince James. Characterised by an ineptitude that proved fatal, the rebellion came to a virtual halt with defeats at Preston and Sheriffmuir near Stirling, and by the time James disembarked at Peterhead it was all over bar the shouting. The 'Old Pretender', as he came to be known, quickly departed again for France. Another equally incompetent invasion, this one sponsored by Spain, foundered on the west coast of Scotland in 1719.

One of the many memorial stones on the battlefield of Culloden. The site of the Jacobite defeat in April 1746 is owned by the National Trust for Scotland, has an excellent visitor centre, and is a popular tourist attraction.

Bonnie Prince Charlie.

Then came the Jacobite Rebellion of 1745, subject of thousands of books and a romantic aura that refuses to go away despite the less-than-glamorous reality of the campaign. The romance is entirely due to James II's grandson Charles, a good-looking and charismatic youth with surprisingly effective leadership qualities. Deprived of a promised French invasion fleet, Charles recklessly landed in the Hebrides with just two ships and seven companions: it was mission impossible, but somehow 'Bonnie Prince Charlie' raised the support of the clans and, against all the odds, there was soon a Highland Jacobite army advancing on Edinburgh, and easily defeating a government army at the Battle of Prestonpans in East Lothian.

The military achievements of the 'Young Pretender' were indeed astonishing, and remain an object lesson in how a highly motivated force can succeed in unlikely circumstances. The army swept down through England and in theory could have attacked London. Beset by internal problems, however, the Jacobites turned back at Derby and embarked on what was effectively a long retreat back to the Highlands.

On 17 January 1746, the Hanoverian army that had been pursuing them for weeks finally caught up with the Jacobites. It was a salutary experience for both sides.

The field of combat was a piece of sloping moorland near the central Scottish town of Falkirk. The weather was so bad – blinding snow and fierce, freezing rain – that neither side could see what was happening, and the cannon were not brought into play because they were stuck in the sodden ground. This was the reality of a typical eighteenth-century pitched battle – mud, poor visibility, cold and chaos.

The Jacobite commander, Lord George Murray – a superb battlefield tactician and the actual hero of the campaign – marched his Highlanders towards the government lines at such a pace that his opposite number, Lieutenant General Henry Hawley, at first refused to believe the advance was actually happening. As the Jacobites broke into a run – the famous Highland Charge, an unstoppable downhill tornado of muscle and edged steel – Hawley unleashed his dragoons, supposedly a battle-winning tactic. Disembowelling and blinding the horses as they ran, the clansmen utterly disrupted the

In contrast, the Jacobite victory at the Battle of Falkirk in January 1746 is almost unknown; the only marker is this monument on a minor road, while the battlefield itself is farmland.

cavalry charge, and soon the panicked mounts and riders were trampling over their own infantry in their need to escape. It was a rout.

This, however, was on the south flank. To the north, protected by a small ravine, the government forces stood their ground and repulsed the Highland Charge. At this point, the victorious Jacobites to the south should have wheeled round to the left and attacked the redcoats from the rear. But the clan warriors, terrifying en masse, were not trained with the discipline of regular troops – they continued to pursue the fleeing soldiers within their sights, rather than helping their fellows. The government forces could have pressed home their advantage at this point – but darkness fell. At dawn the Jacobites were astonished to discover that they had in fact won the battle, having killed around 300 Hanoverians in contrast to fifty of their own losses.

Muddy, grim and confusing, with no hint of dark glamour, the Battle of Falkirk has not received very much attention from popular history, but this neglect is unjustified. For although the government army had lost, keen minds had been studying the Jacobite tactics. By the time of the Battle of Culloden in April, the Hanoverian troops had been drilled in a new form of close-combat warfare, in which tight ranks and the fixed bayonet played a major part. Culloden saw the utter extinction of the Jacobite dream and unleashed a wave of terror on the Highlands, but it was ironically at the victory of Falkirk that the weaknesses of the Jacobites were fatally exposed.

Here's a coda to warm the flintiest of hearts: after the result at Falkirk was known, Sir John Cope, the losing general at the Battle of Prestonpans, collected £10,000 – about £850,000 in today's value. Having seen the Jacobites in action, he guessed that the next clash between the two sides would result in a government defeat – and so he placed a bet to that effect against his own side. Lovely.

INVASION! (FRENCH STYLE)

'The best thing I know between France and England is – the sea.'

Douglas William Jerrold, The Anglo-French Alliance, 1859

It's entirely possible you've never heard of the Battle of Tory Island. Yet this decisive naval action, in which the Royal Navy took seven enemy ships, killed 700 men and captured four times that number, marked the last stage in a protracted attempt at invasion by France – not from across the Channel, but from Britain's 'soft white underbelly' – Ireland and the west.

Britain's troops and navy tended to be concentrated in the south and east, the coasts facing the Continent. Wales and Ireland, meanwhile, were relatively poorly defended. In addition, many Irishmen and women were highly disaffected with British rule: if a foreign power could land a force and link up with an Irish rebellion, Ireland might serve as a springboard for the invasion of Wales and north-west and south-west England. At least, that was the plan.

INVASION PART 1

December 1796. The French Revolution of 1789 and the subsequent execution of King Louis XVI in January 1793 sent shockwaves through the monarchies of Europe. By the spring of 1793, Great Britain was at war with the new French Republic. The first French invasion attempt took place in December 1796, when some forty-five ships left the port of Brest in the far west of France and circled round to Bantry Bay in the south-west of Ireland. The plan was to land 15,000 battle-hardened troops, link up with a rebellion fomented by the Society of United Irishman under their leader Wolfe Tone, rout the dispersed British forces, and take Dublin within two weeks. From there, a more concentrated invasion would target Wales. In a virtual repeat of the Spanish Armada debacle 200 years earlier, however, the French fleet was defeated by the Atlantic gales. No landing was possible, and more than 2,200 soldiers and sailors lost their lives, the majority not to the (largely ineffective) Royal Navy response, but to storms and shipwreck. In total, twelve ships were lost and the invasion and rebellion were both abandoned.

INVASION PART 2

February 1797. A few weeks later the French were back again, this time successfully landing near Fishguard on the west coast of Wales. The make-up of the small invasion force was typical of the period: their leader was an Irish-American who had fought against the British in the American War of Independence, the officers were a mix of French and Irish, and the troops consisted of both veteran soldiers and 'irregulars' – a euphemism for a ragbag of political prisoners from the defeated Royalist regime in France, deserters, and hardcore criminals. Many of the latter became drunk on plundered wine and simply abandoned the fight. Within two days, the 'Battle of Fishguard' was over, with around thirty casualties on the French side. It is often said to be the last successful attempt by an invasion force to land on the British mainland.

INVASION PART 3

October 1797. Another invasion attempt took place nine months later. At the time, the Netherlands was under French occupation. The Dutch fleet set sail for the English Channel, intending to link up with the French at Brest and launch a combined assault on the west of Ireland. Unfortunately for the Dutch, they were spotted by a British fleet in the North Sea and defeated at the Battle of Camperdown on 11 October 1797. Deprived of their ally's strength, the French fleet never left port and, once again, the invasion came to naught.

INVASION PART 4

August 1798. In May 1798, a widespread rebellion broke out in Ireland. Encouraged by this strategic opportunity, the French tried again and in August this time successfully landed troops at Killala in County Mayo, in the west of Ireland. A few days later, a combined French and Irish force defeated the British Army at the nearby Battle of Castlebar, but in early September the British won a crushing victory at the Battle of Ballinamuck in the east of Ireland. Although the captured French were repatriated, the rebels were treated with great brutality, the campaign of sword, fire and rope a mirror image of the horrors inflicted on the Scottish Highlands following the Jacobite Rebellion fifty years earlier.

INVASION PART 5

September 1798. In August, the French had reached Killala without incident. This first force had been relatively modest, but on 16 September a larger expedition was mounted, again confident of reaching north-west Ireland without being bothered by the Royal Navy. At this point, the French did not know that the Irish rebellion had been defeated, and that their own forces in Ireland had already surrendered. As the French ships approached the coast in the vain hope of a landing, they were surprised by a much larger British fleet – this time the Royal Navy had been more vigilant.

The battle took place near Tory Island, off the north-west coast of Donegal, on 12 October. The French flagship *Hoche* was repeatedly raked with close-quarter cannon fire and after two hours of hellish bombardment finally surrendered, having suffered high casualties. Other French ships progressively surrendered as they were worn down by the superior British firepower. After a full day's battle, several French vessels slipped away, some of which were later captured – including the *Résolue*, which allowed HMS *Melampus* to come up alongside in the mistaken impression that she was a French ship. The *Résolue*'s captain only realised his error when *Melampus* opened fire at point-blank range. In total, 70 per cent of the invasion force was lost, a veritable catastrophe that, combined with the crushing of the earlier landing force, put an end to French attempts to use Ireland as their invasion platform. The brutal suppression in the aftermath of the rebellion, plus the capture of Wolfe Tone aboard the *Hoche* (he later committed suicide), also removed Ireland as a strategic partner for the French. It seemed as if France was going to have to face up to its failures, and forget about invading Britain.

But then an ambitious and brilliant general, flush with his victories right across Europe, turned his eyes to the unconquered nation across the Channel. His name: Napoleon Bonaparte.

INVASION! (NAPOLEONIC STYLE)

'France ... must destroy the English monarchy, or expect itself to be destroyed by these intriguing and enterprising islanders ... Let us concentrate all our efforts on the navy and annihilate England. That done, Europe is at our feet.'

Napoleon Bonaparte, 1797

Had you been in the region of Boulogne in 1803, you would have been witness to an extraordinary sight: an army 200,000-strong, camped around a harbour filled with 2,000 boats. Like Hitler in 1940, Napoleon was planning a massive amphibious invasion of the south of England.

Dover Castle, the key to holding the road to London. (LOC, LC-DIG-ppmsc-08353)

Contemporary British cartoon mocking French delusions: Napoleon and Josephine feast on England whilst, in the background, the writing is on the wall. (LOC, LC-USZC4-8790)

Twenty-two miles across the Channel on the White Cliffs of Dover, the French invasion forces could be easily observed. The British response was to militarise the South Coast on a scale that would not be replicated until the Second World War. Volunteer militias – the Napoleonic-era equivalent of Dad's Army – were formed in every county. Beaches and other likely landing points were defended by 103 Martello Towers – fortified gun platforms with long-range cannon. A 28-mile-long canal was erected across the low-lying Romney Marshes in Kent and East Sussex, its purpose to act as a defensive moat. The strategic lynchpin of Chatham and the River Medway was strengthened by additional forts. And at Dover itself, one of the most astonishing military structures of all time was constructed – the Grand Shaft.

White Cliffs of Dover, from where an invading army could easily be sighted. (LOC, LC-DIG-ppmsc-08355)

Dover had for centuries been regarded as the 'key to England', because of its safe harbour and commanding castle. The problem was that the technology of war had outpaced the old ways. If the Western Heights above the castle were occupied, the enemy's artillery could pound the medieval structure to bits – and the road to London would be open. The solution hit upon was to pre-empt this by turning the Western Heights into a veritable fortress, defended against attack from both land and sea, and mounting one of the most formidable artillery arrays in Europe. In addition, a cylindrical shaft 140ft deep was bored down through the cliff from the Western Heights to the harbour. Fitted with three staircases, the Grand Shaft allowed the rapid deployment of troops to wherever the enemy was concentrated.

As it turned out, none of these staggeringly costly defences were put to the test – and if they had, it is questionable how long they could have held out against Napoleon, the acknowledged 'lord of war'. After a truly stellar career as a general, Napoleon had seized power in France in 1799, five years later upgrading his common-garden status of dictator to that of nothing less than emperor. He was a master at winning land battles. Both sides, however, recognised that the crucial factor in invading island Britain was the Royal Navy. Napoleon's elaborate plan was to send French ships to the West Indies as a diversionary feint. The British home fleet would then sail west to defend what they thought

British cartoon of the era showing what 'John Bull' had planned for Napoleon when he arrived. (LC-USZ62-112)

Napoleon in typical battle-winning style.

was an attack on vital colonial possessions in the Caribbean, but the French ships would slip back to Europe, take command of the Channel and escort the vast flotilla over from Boulogne.

Many years later, when Napoleon was on his final exile on the island of St Helena in the South Atlantic, his doctor was Barry O'Meara, a British naval surgeon. In 1817 O'Meara quizzed the ex-emperor on his former invasion plans. Napoleon revealed his intentions had been:

> ... to land near Sheerness and Chatham, and to push directly for London where I calculated to arrive in four days. During the march, I would have made my army observe the most exemplary discipline, marauding or otherwise injuring or insulting the inhabitants would have been punished with instant death. I would have published a proclamation ... declaring that we were only come as friends to the English nation, to render them free and to relieve them from an obnoxious and despotical aristocracy, whose object was to keep them eternally at war in order to enrich themselves and their families at the expense of the blood of the people. Arrived at London I would have proclaimed a Republic ... Liberty, Equality, Sovereignty of the people, abolished the Monarchical Government, the nobility and the House of Peers, the House of Commons I would have retained with a great reform, the property of the nobles I would have declared to be forfeited and to be divided amongst the people.

Napoleon's plans of conquest faltered at the first hurdle: the French fleets failed to fully escape the British naval blockade and the Caribbean diversion was a non-starter. The ships that returned to France were then defeated by the British at the Battle of Cape Finisterre. This was the middle of 1805 – the troops at Boulogne had by now been encamped for twenty unproductive and bored months. Deprived of his naval support, Napoleon rerouted his vast army and marched it into Germany for a new (and typically very successful) land-based campaign. Less than two months later, the French fleet was decisively defeated by Admiral Lord Nelson at the Battle of Trafalgar. Although the possibility of invasion continued until 1812, the crisis of 1803–05 – when invasion was expected on an almost daily basis – was over.

HMS *Victory*, Nelson's flagship; he died aboard this ship, along with more than fifty of his crew, before the battle was won. (LC-DIG-ppmsc-08801)

Napoleon was finally defeated near the Belgian village of Waterloo in 1815, his capture marking the end of the most successful and extensive (not to mention ruthless) military career since, say, Alexander the Great or Genghis Khan.

Britain was fortunate indeed that Bonaparte's iron legions did not cross the Channel. The Napoleonic Wars had encompassed dozens of countries, including modern-day Austria, Belgium, the Czech Republic, Denmark, Egypt, Finland, Germany, Hungary, Italy, Luxembourg, Malta, the Netherlands, Norway, Poland, Portugal, Russia, Slovakia, Spain, Sweden, Switzerland, Turkey and others. Large areas of Europe were devastated. Conflicts also took place across the globe, from the Caribbean to Africa and the Pacific, while in 1812, the United States of America was briefly at war on the side of France against Great Britain.

Between 1803 and 1815, somewhere between 2.5 and 3.5 million soldiers and sailors died, while civilian casualties accounted for another 1–3 million deaths. Perhaps 6 million corpses: Napoleon can be said to have instituted the first true world war.

21 October 1805 – the Royal Navy defeats the combined fleets of France and Spain off Cape Trafalgar in the south-west of Spain.

THE PETERLOO MASSACRE

Rise like Lions after slumber
In unvanquishable number,
Shake your chains to earth like dew
Which in-sleep had fallen on you –
Ye are many – they are few.

Shelley, The Mask of Anarchy, 1819
(Not published until 1832 because of the libel laws)

Fifteen people killed. 654 wounded, the majority of them seriously, slashed with sabres, beaten with batons, or trampled by horses. And a day that (eventually) changed British democracy forever. That was the result of a political rally at St Peter's Field in Manchester – what, in reference to the Battle of Waterloo in 1815, became dubbed the Peterloo Massacre.

One of the reasons Great Britain had won the Napoleonic Wars was because it was the most industrialised nation in Europe. Its mills, factories and iron foundries could turn out the materials and weapons needed to wage a long war, and turn them out faster and more efficiently than other less industrialised countries. As a consequence, British society was changing, with the rise of something never seen before: a large industrial population, an urban working class whose numbers were beginning to challenge the traditional stranglehold on power of the landowning classes. In particular, the parliamentary system was well behind the times: many large industrial cities like Manchester had no MPs, and the overwhelming majority of the population had neither the vote nor an elected representative in the House of Commons.

Added to this irresistible social and economic change was the fiery charge supplied by the American and French Revolutions of 1776 and 1789 respectively. The first showed that British sovereignty could be overthrown, and the second demonstrated that the lower orders could overcome and even dispose of a king: both were living proof that countries could be run as republics and not monarchies. For the British Establishment, such ideas were terrifying – and so ensued the long affray between the supporters of the status quo, and a diverse and variable Radical

The Peterloo Massacre! Down with 'im! Chop 'im down, my brave boys!'

opposition, some of whom wanted reform, while others hankered after revolution.

To make matters worse, Britain did not yet have a civilian police force. The only way to quell discontent, and the only way to ensure that the law was enforced, was to send in the army. This was one thing during the Middle Ages, when hacking and slashing at revolting peasants was all in a day's work for a fragile monarchy and a feudal aristocracy; it was another thing entirely for an industrialised and urban modern nation.

On 16 August 1819, some 50,000–60,000 people assembled in an open space at Manchester as one of a series of meetings calling for increased representation. A number of earlier Radical plots and 'risings' – some of which had actually been instigated by government *agents provocateurs* – had made the authorities nervous, and large numbers of soldiers were on hand, including an artillery team with two 6-pounder guns. As the meeting started, the magistrates issued an order for the arrest of the principal speaker, Henry Hunt. Realising that an arrest could not be easily made on a platform surrounded by the largest crowd anyone had ever seen, they sent in the mounted troops of the Manchester and Salford Yeomanry, who, crucially, were not professional soldiers, but enthusiastic amateurs.

What happened next depends on who you read. One version has it that the undisciplined cavalry, unable to make headway through the dense mass, started laying about them with their sabres. Another version is that people in the crowd started throwing missiles at the riders and attacking their horses. Whatever made things actually kick off, blood was soon flowing. As Samuel Bamford wrote in his book *Passages in the Life of a Radical*: 'Their sabres were plied to hew a way through naked held-up hands, and defenceless heads; and then chopped limbs, and wound gaping skulls were seen; and groans and cries were mingled with the din of that horrid confusion.' The yeomanry cut their way to the platform and indiscriminately attacked and arrested as many people as they could get their hands on. As the crowd started to fight back, the professional cavalry of the 15th Hussars charged the crowd, while bayonet-wielding infantry blocked the escape routes.

The violence went well beyond mere crowd control. The yeomanry deliberately targeted women, including those who were obviously pregnant or carrying babes in arms. For months, anti-Radical propaganda had portrayed female reformers as unnatural and monstrous, neglectful wives and mothers, whores, or subhuman creatures: this misogynistic violence was the payoff. Women made up just one-eighth of the crowd, but accounted for a third of the total casualties.

It is quite likely that some of the injuries were never reported, as admitting that you had attended the meeting could have severe consequences.

Weaver James Lees suffered two severe sabre cuts to his head, but was turned away from the infirmary because he refused to condemn the Radicals. Hugh Birley, a local factory owner, was the leader of the yeoman cavalry: when he found out that William Marsh had been at the assembly – something obvious from Marsh's sabre wound and horse-trampled broken leg – he immediately sacked Marsh's three children. Hatter Jonathan Clarke, severely disabled during the attack and thus unable to work and pay rent, was branded a reformer by his landlord and, along with his wife and seven children, turned out of his home.

The consequences of the massacre were not immediate. There was no official inquiry and the government remained utterly unapologetic, even triumphant. Radicals were prosecuted (and some, especially the women, very badly treated), while none of the soldiers were ever brought to book for their crimes. Pro-Radical accounts of the events were curtailed by the oppressive libel laws, with booksellers prosecuted for 'bringing the soldiers of Our Lord the King into discredit and disgrace by charging them with murder and cruelties'. The cause of reform did not advance, and it was another thirteen years before a very limited parliamentary reform finally took place.

Eventually, however, the massacre found its place in the rhetoric of the organised working class demonstrations of later generations. 'Remember Peterloo!' cried the banners, and, while other episodes in the long class war were forgotten, the events of 16 August 1819 became enshrined in the national consciousness: the Peterloo Massacre is now as much part of our heritage as the Battle of Waterloo.

ASSASSINS' CREED

'it is worth being shot at to see how much one is loved.'

Queen Victoria, 1882

In 1865, John Wilkes Booth killed Abraham Lincoln, President of the United States of America, with a single shot to the back of the head from a .44 Derringer pistol. In 1881, Charles J. Guiteau fired two fatal shots with a .442 snubnose Webley Bulldog revolver at President James Garfield. Assassins were also active in Britain at the period – but the would-be killers of Queen Victoria were of an entirely different calibre.

Queen Victoria, shortly after her marriage.

Attempt No. 1: June 1840

The perpetrator: 18-year-old Edward Oxford, an unemployed former bar worker.

The events: The young queen and her husband of four months liked to take a late afternoon ride on Constitution Hill near Buckingham Palace in an open carriage, accompanied by only two outriders. Oxford fired two pistols in succession at Victoria: both missed, partly because Prince Albert pushed his wife's head down.

The outcome: Oxford was found not guilty by reason of insanity. No bullets were ever found and Oxford had probably not loaded his weapons with anything other than a small charge of gunpowder. After twenty-seven years as a model prisoner in asylums, he was released on condition he emigrated to Australia.

Curious facts: Victoria and Albert made sure that the public could see that the queen was both unharmed and unfazed, and recent criticisms of the monarchy were swept aside in a wave of royalist enthusiasm.

Attempt No. 2: May 1842

The perpetrator: 20-year-old tradesman John Francis.

The events: On 30 May, a man standing at almost the exact same spot as Edward Oxford aimed a pistol at the royal carriage. Either it misfired, or he did not actually pull the trigger. The following day, the queen and Prince Albert took the same route, this time with plain-clothes policemen scattered round the park. Francis appeared and fired – so close that Victoria had heard the click of the hammer – and was instantly apprehended. No one could tell whether the pistol had actually been loaded.

The outcome: Francis was found guilty of high treason and sentenced to be hanged, beheaded, and quartered. The sentence was commuted to hard labour in a Tasmanian penal colony.

Curious facts: This is the moment that truly established Victoria's reputation for courage: she and Albert were determined to flush out the would-be assassin, and so deliberately put themselves in the firing line on the second day.

John Francis' second attempt on the life of Queen Victoria.

Attempt No. 3: July 1842

The perpetrator: 17-year-old John William Bean.

The events: Bean fired a pistol loaded with only paper and tobacco at the queen.

The outcome: Described as a miserable-looking man whose hunched back meant he was barely above 4ft tall, Bean was sentenced to a mere eighteen months. He spent the rest of his life in obscurity, working as a news vendor – instead of headlining newspapers, he was selling them.

Curious facts: It was probably around this time that Prince Albert presented his wife with a parasol lined with chain mail – to act as a shield. It is not clear whether she ever used it.

Attempt No. 4: May 1849

The perpetrator: 25-year-old William Hamilton. Hamilton's life had largely consisted of near-starvation in Ireland during the Potato Famine, followed by near-starvation in London. Not surprisingly, he was a very angry man.

The events: The venue was Constitution Hill once more. Again it was a lone gunman. And again the firearm was not loaded.

The outcome: Hamilton spent five years on a prison hulk in Gibraltar and served the last part of his seven-year sentence in Western Australia.

Curious facts: Hamilton first tried to build his own gun out of wood and the spout of a tea-kettle. When this proved ineffective, he borrowed a pistol from his landlady, who after the trial was offered the enormous sum of £40 for it by a souvenir hunter.

Attempt No. 5: June 1850

The perpetrator: 31-year-old Robert Pate, a well-off former army officer.

The events: Pate, who had been displaying signs of mental illness for some time, came up to the queen's carriage in Piccadilly and struck her hard on the head with his brass-tipped walking cane.

The outcome: Pate pleaded guilty and spent seven years in a penal colony in Tasmania.

Curious facts: On the evening of the assault, Victoria arrived at the Royal Opera House with a black eye and bruised face. The entire audience applauded her and the cast interrupted the play to sing a collective 'God Save the Queen' on stage.

William Hamilton has a go at assassinating the queen – or not, as the gun was unloaded.

Attempt No. 6: February 1872

The perpetrator: 17-year-old Arthur O'Connor, who seems to have suffered florid delusions.

The events: O'Connor approached the royal carriage waving a pistol and a piece of paper he wanted the queen to sign, freeing Irish political prisoners. Victoria's Scottish servant John Brown intervened.

The outcome: O'Connor was birched and given a year's imprisonment.

Curious facts: O'Connor later wrote to the queen asking to be appointed Poet Laureate.

Attempt No. 7: March 1882

The perpetrator: 28-year-old Roderick Maclean.

The events: Of all the attempts, this was the most serious. From a distance of 15yds, Maclean fired a loaded revolver directly at the queen.

The outcome: Maclean, who believed he was the victim of a giant conspiracy and was probably schizophrenic, was found 'not guilty but insane' and spent the rest of his life in Broadmoor.

Curious facts: Victoria was incensed at the verdict, as in her eyes Maclean was clearly guilty. With her usual determination, she had the law changed so that defendants could be found 'guilty but insane'.

Political assassination was a reality in nineteenth-century Britain. In 1812, Prime Minister Spencer Perceval was murdered in the House of Commons by disaffected merchant John Bellingham. In 1843, Daniel M'Naughten shot and killed civil servant Edward Drummond in the mistaken belief that the private secretary was Prime Minister Sir Robert Peel himself. And in 1868 Prince Alfred, Victoria's second son, was shot and wounded in the back by Henry O'Farrell while visiting Australia. Fortunately for Queen Victoria, her own would-be assassins were ill-favoured when it came to anything approaching competence.

The assassination of Spencer Perceval, the prime minister, by John Bellingham.

'An evil plexus of slums that hide human creeping things.'

Arthur Morrison describing the East End in Tales of Mean Streets, 1894

There have been tens of thousands of murders in British history. And there have been, gods preserve us, far worse and far more energetic serial killers.

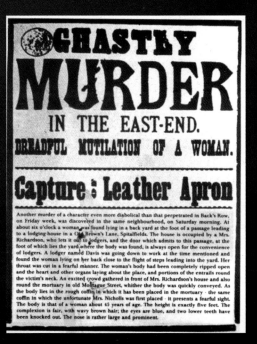

GHASTLY
MURDER
IN THE EAST-END.
DREADFUL MUTILATION OF A WOMAN.

Capture : Leather Apron

Another murder of a character even more diabolical than that perpetrated in Back's Row, on Friday week, was discovered in the same neighbourhood, on Saturday morning. At about six o'clock a woman was found lying in a back yard at the foot of a passage leading to a lodging-house in a Chs Brown's Lane, Spitalfields. The house is occupied by a Mrs. Richardson, who lets it out to lodgers, and the door which admits to this passage, at the foot of which lies the yard, where the body was found, is always open for the convenience of lodgers. A lodger named Davis was going down to work at the time mentioned and found the woman lying on her back close to the flight of steps leading into the yard. Her throat was cut in a fearful manner. The woman's body had been completely ripped open and the heart and other organs laying about the place, and portions of the entrails round the victim's neck. An excited crowd gathered in front of Mrs. Richardson's house and also round the mortuary in old Montague Street, whither the body was quickly conveyed. As the body lies in the rough coffin in which it has been placed in the mortuary · the same coffin in which the unfortunate Mrs. Nicholls was first placed · it presents a fearful sight. The body is that of a woman about 45 years of age. The height is exactly five feet. The complexion is fair, with wavy brown hair; the eyes are blue, and two lower teeth have been knocked out. The nose is rather large and prominent.

A wanted poster issued during the search for Jack the Ripper.

And yet, while many of the details of these gruesome acts are lost except to those who take an interest in such matters, the name Jack the Ripper is to this day on everyone's lips. Even those who have no interest in crime or murder know his name. Or, rather they don't know his name: for the Ripper's universal fame lies on the simple fact that not only was he was never caught, he was never even identified. Saucy Jack, Red Jack, Leather Apron, Jack from Hell – his nicknames simply emphasise the reality that the identity of this killer and mutilator of women is a mystery: and there's nothing we like more than a mystery.

Between 31 August and 9 November 1888, 'Jack' murdered five women: Mary Ann Nichols, Annie Chapman, Elizabeth Stride, Catherine Eddowes and Mary Kelly. All were mutilated in the most appalling manner, with body parts removed and theatrically staged in or around the corpse. Some organs appear to have been taken as souvenirs. Two of the victims were murdered on the same night, 30 September. The principal weapon appears to have been a long, sharp knife – perhaps more than one.

The Whitechapel where Saucy Jack disembowelled and cut up his victims was the Whitechapel where the average number of people living in a small unheated, unfurnished room was seven; where twopence bought you a night sleeping upright against a rope in an overcrowded and vermin-infested dosshouse; where child prostitution, rape and incest were widespread; where 55 per cent of children did not see their fifth birthday; where liquid sewage slopped through cellars and streets; where closely packed filthy tenements crabbed against a labyrinth of alleys and tiny courtyards; where blood and excrement from the slaughterhouses poured over the pavements; and where every form of disease, crime, neglect, violence and horror were commonplace. It was, in short, a nightmare to police. Most crimes went unreported, and there was a universal hatred of any kind of authority. In the past year, thousands of the destitute and desperate had squatted in Trafalgar Square, to be violently cleared by a combined police and military operation. Demonstrations were becoming more frequent, and more truculent. Policemen's heads were broken and property damaged. The year 1887 had been marked by nationwide celebrations for Queen Victoria's Jubilee – but the East End might as well have been on another planet.

All the Ripper's victims were prostitutes. There were perhaps 1,200 low-class streetwalking prostitutes in Whitechapel at that time, with the figure for the whole of London around 80,000. It was estimated that 15 per cent of women in the East End

Trafalgar Square: in this era, thousands of destitute squatters were forcibly removed by the police. (LC-DIG-ppmsc-08573)

and prostitution was often the only way a woman could earn a piece of bread or a bed for the night. Films about the Ripper often portray his victims as glamorous, even sexy, young women. Nichols was 43, Chapman 47; Stride 45 and Eddowes 46. Gin, poor diet and atrocious living conditions had long removed any hint of sexual allure. Even the youngest and most attractive, 25-year-old Kelly, had the air of a hefty wrestler. The crimes clearly

Dorset Street, Spitalfields. Miller's Court, where Mary Kelly was murdered, is on the left, by the carriages.

rgans were targeted, along with other parts – ut there is no evidence that the killer had any kind f conventional sexual interest in the women.

The murders convulsed London in a way that one had done before: not just because they were ickeningly anatomical, not just because they vere repeated, but because they sold newspapers. n the eighteenth century, only toffs subscribed to ewspapers, or went to upmarket coffee houses to ead them. By the 1880s, a great many ordinary obs required a degree of literacy; as reading ecame more widespread, so new markets opened.

Publications aimed at the middle classes boomed and then it was realised that many working people also had an avid interest in news. Newspapers that had previously had print runs in the hundreds were now being pressed in the tens of thousands and sold in the streets to ordinary people. Competition was cut-throat, with journalists vying to outdo each other with scams, tricks and scoops, sometimes inventing news items, or embellishing existing stories so they had a longer shelf life. And Jack the Ripper was journalism gold: every new murder, every new suspect, every wrong-footed

Newspaper seller in London. (LOC, LC-DIG-ggbain-08595)

DR. NEILL CREAM'S PILL CASE.
(Black Museum.)

Dr Cream's poison.

move by the police – it was all written down and printed as it happened, enveloping the entire newspaper-reading population in the breathless excitement of an ongoing investigation, while a monster stalked the streets of darkest London. But then the murders stopped, and the murderer escaped both justice and identification. This is the reason why Jack is famous: because he remains a mystery, and because he was the first serial killer of the newspaper age.

Less than four years after the 'terrible autumn' of 1888, Dr Thomas Neill Cream murdered, like the Ripper, five London prostitutes, although his choice of weapon was the poison strychnine and not a knife. Cream's name is in the hall of infamy of serial killers, and there have been fine books written about his crimes – yet most people today have never heard of him.

But we all remember Jack.

AD 1911

THE SIEGE OF SIDNEY STREET

'Nothing like it had ever happened before in the history of the Met.'

The Official Encyclopedia of Scotland Yard, *1999*

Britain had never seen anything like it, and the Metropolitan Police were taken by complete surprise. As the extraordinary events of 3 January 1911 spun out, they encompassed armed police, army sharp-shooters, field artillery, the fire brigade, thousands of Londoners – and an ambitious young Home Secretary by the name of Winston Churchill.

The events had actually begun on 16 December 1910, when a group of Latvian immigrants were disturbed trying to break into Harris' jewellers' shop in the Houndsditch area of Whitechapel. They had rented the building which backed onto the rear of the shop, but the robbery was under-taken on the Friday night, in a predominately Jewish area. The unexpected noises on the eve of the Jewish Sabbath alerted the neighbours, and nine policemen arrived. In the ensuing melee, three of the unarmed officers, Sergeants Bentley and Tucker and Constable Choate, were killed by gunshots, while two more of their colleagues were wounded. The gang also accidentally shot their leader, George Gardstein, who died from his injury the following day. Not surprisingly, a national manhunt for the murderers ensued, and several members of the gang were arrested.

The late nineteenth century and early twentieth century was an era of titanic struggle between entrenched power and new emerging social groups in Europe. Nowhere was this struggle more intense than Tsarist Russia, where a reactionary monarchy and a terrifying secret police attempted to suppress any kind of dissent, whether that dissent took the form of local independence from the tentacles of the vast Russian territory, Communism, Anarchism, or simply standing up for basic human rights. Inevitably this struggle spilled over into neighbouring countries and then the rest of Europe as both refugees and political opponents fled successive persecutions. Many of these exiles came to Britain, which, despite its massive class issues, remained relatively stable. When Karl Marx came to London in 1850, he was amazed to find that British policemen did not carry arms, did not habitually engage in arbitrary torture, and – at least outside the criminal rookeries – were actually quite popular. Many overseas governments and visitors were astonished that Britain tolerated so many foreign 'troublemakers' on its soil, but for most of the Victorian and Edwardian eras, the country remained largely indifferent to the panoply of revolutionary 'isms'. The Houndsditch gang were Latvian anarchists on the run from the tsar's harsh regime, and their robberies were supposedly 'expropriations' designed to fund their resistance activities, but, like many violent political groups today, simple criminal greed seems to have overtaken their ideological principles.

Late on 2 January 1911, the police received a tip-off that two of the Houndsditch murderers were hiding out on the second floor of No. 100 Sidney Street in Stepney. By 4.45 a.m. the following day, the fourteen occupants of the house had been evacuated and the area was cordoned off. At dawn, the police attempted an entry, only to be repulsed by heavy gunfire from advanced Mauser pistols. One detective was wounded and was taken away on a stretcher across the only route out of the line of fire – across the roof. More gunfire pinned down other officers, who, armed with an impromptu arsenal of Bulldog revolvers, shotguns and .22 rifles, found themselves outgunned and outranged.

No one had anticipated that the gang, surrounded and with no possibility of escape, would make a death or glory last stand. A request

Churchill at the Siege of Sidney Street.

for help went up through the police hierarchy to Home Secretary Winston Churchill, who authorised the use of troops, and then turned up to excitedly direct operations on the ground himself – an overturning of the usual arms-length relationship between the police and their overall boss. At 10.45 a.m., twenty-one marksmen of the Scots Guards took up various positions on a nearby roof, within shop doorways, and lying prone on newspaper hoardings in the street.

Faced with this withering fire, the gunmen retreated from the second storey and attic to the lower floors. Even so, they were not giving up, and Churchill ordered up heavier firepower – a Maxim gun (a heavy automatic machine gun, later a mainstay of the slaughter of the First World War) and even field artillery. As it happened, none of this additional ordinance was required. A fire broke out in the building from an unknown source (perhaps the gunmen were burning incriminating papers) and by 1.30 p.m., flames and smoke were pouring out. Churchill forbade the fire brigade to go in, probably a good thing as shots continued to be heard for another half an hour. Eventually the fire gutted No. 100. Two bodies were found – one gunman had been shot on the first floor, while his companion had succumbed to the smoke on the ground floor. In the proceedings to make the building safe, a fireman died from a collapsing wall.

One of the extraordinary elements of the Sidney Street Siege was that much of it was captured on newsreel, and the immediacy of the events is powerful even today. You also get a sense of how much of a public spectacle the siege was – a huge crowd of many thousands was present, kept back by a cordon of 500 uniformed and mounted police.

Apart from the deceased George Gardstein and the two men killed at Sidney Street – Fritz Svaars and William Sokolow – the Houndsditch gang comprised five men and two women. Unbelievably, none were convicted for the murders of the police officers, a failure put down to the difficulty of successfully prosecuting a group of people who could not speak English and whose witness statements were contradictory and confusing for juries. In 1973, police officer and author Donald Rumbelow examined the archives and concluded that the principal perpetrator at Houndsditch was Jacob Peters. After his acquittal, Peters bigamously married a middle-class English woman, and then returned to Russia in 1917 to take part in the Revolution. The next year, as deputy head of the secret police, the unrepentant murderer of policemen moved up the ladder, bloodily eliminating whoever was enemy of the week in the endless purges of the Soviet Union.

In Britain, the siege prompted the upgrading of the weaponry available to armed police in emergency situations. As for Churchill, his highly unconventional actions earned him a dressing-down from his colleagues – and a stray bullet through his top hat on the day.

AD 1915

DEATH FROM THE SKIES – ZEPPELIN!

'Bombs away.'

People sleeping in the London Underground. Children evacuated from the cities. Blackouts. Buildings ablaze at night. Searchlights. Barrage balloons. Anti-aircraft flak. Heavy bombers tangling with fighter aircraft. Burning aircraft plunging to earth. Mass civilian casualties. This, you think, is the Blitz of 1940–41, the abiding image of the Home Front in the Second World War. But these horrors of death from the skies were actually first visited on the civilian population much earlier: during the First World War.

Coastal raids aside, most of mainland Britain had not suffered directly during the wars of the nineteenth century, the security of the nation guaranteed by both its island geography and the Royal Navy's command of the seas. That all changed in the First World War: for the first time, enemy flying machines were seen in the skies over Britain, dropping bombs and wreaking havoc – not to mention spreading panic and affecting morale.

The first Zeppelin had flown in 1900. By the outbreak of the war in August 1914, the horrors of aerial bombardment were, courtesy of science-fiction novels, speculative newspaper articles and earlier but false panics, deeply ingrained within the public imagination, and bombing raids were expected to commence almost immediately. The early Zeppelins had a restricted range that meant they could only reach south-east England and the lower reaches of the east coast – but nonetheless, sightings of enemy airships were

First World War poster showing a 'dirigible' caught in the searchlights. (LC-USZC4-10972)

IT IS FAR BETTER TO FACE THE BULLETS THAN TO BE KILLED AT HOME BY A BOMB

JOIN THE ARMY AT ONCE & HELP TO STOP AN AIR RAID

GOD SAVE THE KING

consistently reported from Liverpool and Carlisle, not to mention Highland Scotland and Belfast, all of which were far beyond the capability of even the souped-up Zeppelins of the later war. After this 'scareship' panic, proceedings calmed down – until 19 January 1915, when two Zeppelins dropped a few bombs on Great Yarmouth and King's Lynn in Norfolk, killing four people. The first raid on London took place on 31 May, and on 8 September a single Zeppelin caused an enormous amount of damage in the centre of the city. From now on, large numbers of people in England lived in fear of the silent 'death from above', and up to 300,000 were spending their nights sheltering in the London Underground. From 1916, the first blackouts were imposed.

As the war progressed, Zeppelin technology improved and the targets became more widespread: Folkestone on the South Coast; the armaments factories of Warrington and Birmingham; the ports of Sunderland and Berwick-on-Tweed; and Edinburgh and its port, Leith. The Zeppelins' high flight ceiling and silent approach made detection and protection difficult. Conscious of the raids' effect on public morale, over time the British government diverted large numbers of men and resources from the industrial carnage of the Western Front and the other theatres of war into anti-aircraft gunnery, barrage balloons, radio interception and search-lights. But in 1915–16, the Zeppelins were the rulers of the skies – except for the odd case of chance and extraordinary courage.

I dare say that if you are in a Zeppelin flying thousands of feet above the far-distant ground you do not expect to have bombs rain down on you from above. But that is indeed what happened to Zeppelin LZ.37 on 7 June 1915. The Zeppelin was on its way back from a night-time bombing raid over London. By chance, its path crossed that of Lieutenant Rex Warneford of the Royal Naval Air Service, who had been part of a British air raid launched from a Belgian airfield against the Zeppelin base at Evere near Brussels, in which one airship had been destroyed. Warneford had no guns attached to his monoplane, just a rifle in his cockpit. Driven off by the enemy machine guns, he continued to follow the airship as it slowly climbed to 13,000ft over the Channel. By the time the Zeppelin began its descent towards Evere, Warneford was above it. He flew within 200ft of the huge dirigible and dropped – by hand – six 20-pound bombs on its upper surface. The gas-filled giant caught fire, the explosion almost taking out Warneford's little plane in the process. He landed bumpily behind enemy lines, made emergency repairs, and managed to take off again without being captured. LZ.37, meanwhile, crashed near Ghent: it was the first Zeppelin lost to another aircraft. Warneford was awarded the Victoria Cross. He was killed ten days later.

The lieutenant's lucky fluke aside, it was not until 2 September 1916 that a British fighter finally shot down a Zeppelin. By now fighter aircraft were fitted with new weaponry, including incendiary bullets designed to set fire to the airships' inflammable hydrogen. Another airship fell a fiery victim to the incendiary bullets on 27 November. And on 19 October 1917, three were shot down and two others lost. By this point, the cost of the Zeppelin bombing campaign was causing concern to the German High Command, and the number of raids was being severely reduced compared to the intensity of 1916. The final raid, on 5 August 1918, saw the lead Zeppelin shot down and the death

The Zeppelin L.15, brought down by anti-aircraft fire near the mouth of the Thames on 31 March 1916.

Zeppelin bomb damage, London, 13 October 1915. Fifty-six people were killed and 114 injured during the raid.

of Peter Strasser, the architect and leader of the Zeppelin campaign.

With the Zeppelins starting their slow decline, 1916 saw a new addition to the terror: heavy bombers. On 27 November, a single Gotha biplane dropped six bombs on London, and thereafter the kaiser's 'England Squadron' carried out a series of massed raids on the capital and elsewhere in southern England. The Gothas carried heavier bombs than the Zeppelins, and could cause more damage: on 25 May 1917, twenty-three Gothas killed ninety-three people; two weeks later, fourteen Gothas, dropping bombs from 12,000ft, killed 162 civilians in London, the highest death toll for a single air raid of the war. In total the bombers killed 857 people and wounded 2,908, while all the Zeppelin raids accounted for 556 dead and 1,914 other casualties. From this point of view, the bombers were more than 30 per cent deadlier than the Zeppelins. As 1917 progressed, the Gothas were joined by the even larger Giant biplane bombers, and their bombs, which at the start of the war weighed just a few pounds, were now an incredible 1 tonne in weight. Incendiary bombs were also developed. The silent and ominous Zeppelins may have captured the public imagination, but by 1918 the airships had already been outstripped by the defining technology of the twentieth-century air war: the bomber.

U-BOAT AT SCAPA FLOW

'A magnificent feat of arms'

Winston Churchill on the U-boat sinking of HMS Royal Oak

We tend to think of submarine attacks as taking place underwater, with perhaps just a periscope poking above the surface. But one of the most audacious naval actions of the Second World War was undertaken by a U-boat on the surface, within a few hundred yards of British coastal defences. It was this skill and daring that earned Churchill's bitter admiration.

It was about 1 a.m. on 14 October 1939, a moonless night, but the Northern Lights were bright enough for Lieutenant Gunther Prien, who carefully guided the U47 past a blockship that had been specifically sunk as an anti-submarine defence. The crew held their breath as the U-boat snagged a cable, then let out a silent sigh of relief as the obstruction came free. Another scare came when the headlights of a turning car briefly illuminated the waters, but again the Germans were lucky. Despite the noise of its diesel engines, and being not beneath the waters but on the surface, no one noticed as the submarine entered the eastern part of Scapa Flow, the principal northern base for the Royal Navy.

As luck would have it, most of the capital ships of the Home Fleet were elsewhere that night. Over at the west side of the anchorage, too far for Prien to reach without being detected, was the cruiser HMS *Belfast*, plus a number of destroyers, supply ships and auxiliaries, but to the north was the perfect target: the Royal Sovereign class battleship

U-boat out of water. (LOC, LC-USZ62-93699)

HMS *Royal Oak*, a veteran of the First World War, now principally used as a formidable anti-aircraft platform. Prien fired three torpedoes, one of which caused such minor damage that the crew thought it was just something in the paint locker going pop. U47 now turned around and fired her stern tubes – again with no effect. Another turn, and the reloaded bow tubes were fired again.

Thirteen minutes later, *Royal Oak* rolled over and sank, three explosions having ripped her apart. It was later determined that 833 of the total company of 1,400 died, with many of the survivors owing their lives to the prompt action of the smaller ships nearby. U47, meanwhile, still on the surface, zigzagged its way out of Scapa Flow undetected, and returned to Germany for a hero's welcome from Hitler himself. The Royal Navy had suffered a humiliating and major loss in its own heartland.

Scapa Flow was no stranger to the attentions of the German Unterseebooten. A vast natural anchorage sheltered by the ring of the principal islands of the Orkney archipelago, it had been in use by the Royal Navy since 1905, and became home to the Grand Fleet during the First World War. In November 1914, a U-boat came close to penetrating the defences but was rammed by a minesweeper and forced to surrender. In June 1916, the cruiser HMS *Hampshire* struck a submarine-laid mine off the west coast of Orkney and sank with the loss of 643 men out of 655, one of the victims being Field Marshall Lord Kitchener, Britain's Minister for War and the man whose moustachioed face stared out from all those 'I want YOU'

recruiting posters. And in October 1918, another U-boat entered Scapa Flow. Detected first by hydrophones and then by electrical detector loops on the seabed, the submarine was sunk with all hands by the remote detonation of a controlled mine, the first time this had happened in undersea warfare.

After the Armistice in 1918, seventy-four surrendered German ships were interred in Scapa Flow, maintained under difficult and cramped conditions by crews whose incipient revolutionary Socialism and self-formed Soldiers' Councils made their officer's lives a nightmare. Eventually the crew numbers were greatly reduced, but it became clear from the Armistice discussions at Versailles that the ships were going to be split up among the Allies. At 10.30 a.m. on 21 June 1919, Admiral von Reuter broadcast the signal 'Paragraph eleven', a pre-arranged codeword for captains to scuttle their vessels. All watertight doors, portholes, hatches and valves had already been opened, and by 5 p.m. the vast majority of the pride of the German Navy was lying upside-down at the bottom of Scapa Flow, while others were beached by the surprised Royal Navy. Nine German sailors lost their lives, some drowned, some shot by the British trying to prevent further scuttling – one such victim was the captain of the battleship SMS *Markgraf*. Three battleships (including *Markgraf*), four light cruisers and four destroyers are still there on the seabed, and are popular with divers. The *Royal Oak* still lies in 90ft of water, her position marked by a green buoy. Her outline can be clearly seen from the air when the water is clear. An official war grave, it is prohibited to dive on the wreck without permission.

Three generations of British naval power at Portsmouth. At left, Nelson's flagship HMS *Victory*.
At right, a late nineteenth-century cruiser. And in the centre, a First World War torpedo boat.

In 1939, the destruction of the *Royal Oak* and the ease with which the enemy had both entered and departed Scapa Flow was a wake-up call for the Admiralty and the British Government, especially when the Germans staged a successful air raid on Scapa Flow just two days after the sinking. Boom defences, minefields, underwater detection systems and gun batteries were hastily thrown up and more blockships were sunk. By 1941, Scapa Flow was a veritable fortress, with a permanent garrison of perhaps 40,000 personnel, not counting the crews of the uncountable numbers of warships and merchantmen that sought the sanctuary of the anchorage. The biggest engineering and financial operation, however, was the construction of a series of causeways between the eastern islands around Scapa. These 'Churchill Barriers', as they came to be known, blocked any chance of penetration by U-boat. It is now possible to drive from the Orkney Mainland to the southern islands of Burray and South Ronaldsay – a direct result of Gunther Prien's daring attack in 1939.

DEATH FROM THE SKIES: THE BLITZ

'September 7, 1940. Armageddon Day ... The destruction of London had begun.'

Julian Symons, diary, 1940

A state of war officially existed between Germany and Britain on 3 September 1939. Almost immediately the air-raid sirens droned out, but there were no German aircraft in the skies that day. The first air raid on the British Isles took place on 16 October, with an attack on Royal Navy ships in the Firth of Forth. The cruiser HMS *Southampton* was badly damaged, as was

Exeter's High Street; most of the city centre was levelled during the raids. (LOC. LC-DIG-ppmsc-08363)

Battle of Britain pilots.

the destroyer HMS *Mohawk*, and another cruiser was also hit, albeit less seriously. Sixteen sailors lost their lives, and there were also civilian casualties – but these were victims of 'friendly fire' from the bullets of the Spitfires chasing the bombers across the rooftops of Edinburgh. Two Junkers 88 bombers were shot down that day; a welcome change to earlier events in the south of England, which had seen RAF pilots firing at each other in confusion. The day after the Forth attack, more German bombers targeted Scapa Flow in Orkney.

The first raid on England was a single attack on 3 July 1940, at Maidenhead, with a much larger bombing the following day on Portland. Between 10 July and 7 August, numerous sorties were launched against naval targets and ports. And in the middle of August, the Luftwaffe attempted to destroy the RAF on the ground with a series of enormous raids. Thanks to a combination of superior technology (Spitfires and Hurricanes), radar, and the astonishing bravery of pilots, the Battle of Britain became a symbol of determination and courage that the ensuing decades have failed to tarnish – 'Our Finest Hour'.

All this, however, was just the prelude. Having lost the Battle of Britain, the Germans switched strategy – to the mass night-time bombing of cities. The first raid on London, on 7 September, killed or wounded almost 2,000 people, with the East End being hardest hit. The principal target was the docks, and the flames were soon fed by paint drums, rum and even sugar, which formed floating mats of fire on the Thames. On the ground, the eerie effects of high-explosive bomb-blast were being experienced for the first time – one victim could be ripped apart, while the person adjacent would be unharmed, but absolutely naked, all their clothes having been torn off. People nearby might feel their eyeballs being sucked out as great waves of compression and suction pushed and pulled through the streets. One house might be reduced to matchwood, while next door would be untouched. Similar scenes were enacted over the next fifty-six nights, as wave after wave of German bombers struck the capital. It was the Blitz – the named adapted from the German word used for their rapid advance through Europe – Blitzkrieg, 'lightning war'.

From September 1940 to May 1941, all of Britain's major industrial centres and ports were hit – Birmingham, Bristol, Portsmouth, Southampton, Plymouth, Derby, Hull, Leicester, Sheffield, Liverpool, Manchester, Belfast, Glasgow/Clydebank and many other places. In the third week of September alone there were 1,300 fatalities in London, and another 200 elsewhere. By the time that month of hell came to an end, 6,954 civilians had lost their lives. Across the country, some 200,000 houses were completely wiped off the map, with almost another 4 million suffering damage. Hundreds of thousands of Britons were made homeless. On 14/15 November, Coventry

East End family at dinner after a raid.

St Katherine's Dock, London, burning on the night of 7 September 1940.

was so badly devastated that the Germans coined a new verb – Coventrieren, 'to Coventrate'. On 29 December a firebomb attack on central London almost reached St Paul's Cathedral – but the famous photograph of the great dome rising serene above the flames and smoke became a symbol for the resilience and indomitable spirit of the people of London, and Britain as a whole.

A particularly vicious attack took place on 10 May 1941, killing more than 1,400 civilian Londoners and lighting up the night sky with fires for three days. But then the intensity slackened – Britain

despite all the odds, was still fighting on, and new night-flying aircraft, such as the radar-equipped Beaufighter, were bringing down more and more of the enemy. Soon the Luftwaffe bombers were reassigned to Hitler's new war in Russia, and the Battle, not of Britain but for Britain, was effectively won.

However, the air war over Britain was not over. In March and April 1942, hitherto-untouched cities were hit – Canterbury, York, Norwich, Exeter and Bath. These were known as the 'Baedeker raids,' named on the assumption that the Germans had consulted the well-known guidebooks and

deliberately targeted the country's most historic and beautiful cities. And then, on 13 June 1944, an entirely new terror weapon was unleashed on the population – the buzz bomb. The V1, a pilotless jet-powered flying bomb, was distinguished by the put-put of its engine – and then by fifteen seconds of silence between the fuel running out and the bomb falling to earth. One V1 killed 121 people. Altogether, 6,725 buzz bombs fell on southern England, killing over 6,000 and injuring three times that number. Even more terrifying was the V2, the world's first long-distance rocket weapon. The first V2 of the war fell on west London on 8 September 1944, the explosion attributed in the press to a faulty gas main so not as to spread panic about a weapon that could be launched in northern Europe and reach its target just a few minutes later. In total 1,115 V2s fell on the south of England – almost half in the London area – killing 2,754 civilians and seriously injuring some 6,500.

In all, something like 40,000 civilians died as a result of German bombing during the Second World War.

I was recently asked by someone from overseas why, seventy years on, the British remain so obsessed with the Second World War. The answer is, I contend, quite clear: the odds were against us by a long way, and yet we did not surrender, and we survived. That's a story that never goes out of fashion.

A night time view of Canterbury, targeted by Hitler's bombers. (LOC, LC-DIG-ppmsc-08094)

INVASION! (NAZI STYLE)

'We will fight them on the beaches ... we will never surrender.'

Winston Churchill, 4 June 1940

Hitler's intentions towards Britain largely fell into three phases. The first was Conciliation: a mutual non-aggression agreement would guarantee the freedom of both Great Britain and the British Empire, while leaving Germany to do what she pleased on mainland Europe. When, somewhat to Hitler's amazement, that was rebuffed – as in Churchill's famous speech, quoted above – the second phase was Invasion. This was only ever a practical reality between August and October 1940. The final phase was Annihilation: to militarily overcome British forces and bases wherever they might be, from North Africa and the Mediterranean to the home seas and cities, and to bring the stubborn island nation to its knees by destroying its seagoing supply lines.

As we know, the RAF rather spoiled Hitler's plans by refusing to lose the Battle of Britain. The invasion was consequently called off, as without owning the skies above England, the Germans knew they would be in for a hiding. But, as was acknowledged secretly at the time, and has become widely known since, it was a close-run thing. Had the Luftwaffe managed to sustain their attacks on the airfields and aircraft manufacturing facilities for perhaps as little as ten days longer, the RAF may well have been almost entirely destroyed. And if that had happened, then Britain would have been invaded, and may well have fallen.

The German Army had originally planned multiple landings around East Anglia – good flat tank country, ideal for fast-moving blitzkrieg warfare – but wiser counsels in the navy won out for the shortest possible sea crossing, to Kent and East Sussex. Planned to start on 21 September 1940, Operation Sealion was going to transport something like half a million men across the Channel. Landing on the beaches with their soft sand and pebbles posed something of a problem, so 11,000 horses were to be brought over to drag guns and wagons off the beaches and up the steep roads to the cliff tops.

By this point Britain had undertaken the most extensive programme of fixed defensive works since the building of Hadrian's Wall in the second century. The effectiveness of German tactics in

France, the Low Countries and Scandinavia, however, suggests that, however much these defences might cost the invader dearly, eventually the country would capitulate. And if that happened, there were administrators in the Nazi ministries who had already planned the fine detail of the occupation.

One of the first steps would be the rounding up of all Jews and left-wingers. But there were other targets that were less obvious. The Germans had an abiding distrust of what they termed 'internationalist' organisations, which they seemed to almost regard as secret societies. So the Boy Scouts, the Girl Guides and the Rotary Clubs would be banned, as would the Quakers and even the Salvation Army. The Jehovah's Witnesses would be arrested, and Freemasons – against whom Hitler had conceived an illogical but venomous hatred – would be put down. Most academics in the major universities would be arrested, and indeed there were already personnel files on many of them, compiled by German 'exchange students' in the 1930s – bright young men who were actually fervent Nazis. The entertainment and media industries would be purged, with some individuals singled out for special attention – Noël Coward, for example, was destined for a concentration camp because he was homosexual. The Gestapo had decided to set up offices in London, Birmingham, Bristol, Liverpool, Manchester and Glasgow or Edinburgh, and Goebbels had already concluded that the latter would make a fine 'summer capital'. Overseeing all this, as the Chief of the Security Police in Great Britain, would have been a 31-year-old Nazi zealot named SS Colonel Professor Dr Franz Six, who met every cliché of every evil SS officer you have ever seen, and perhaps worse.

Six was charged with not just hunting down, abducting, torturing and murdering 'enemies of the Reich': he also had a cultural mission. He was to oversee the wholesale looting of works of art and important archives – all of which had already been identified – and also dismantle Nelson's Column

Noel Coward, destined for a concentration camp if Hitler had invaded. (LOC, LC-DIG-ggbain-38534)

from Trafalgar Square and arrange for its re-erection as the centrepiece of Hitler's planned new Berlin. As for literature, the Nazis had already shown themselves to be book-burners, but the list of banned authors went far beyond the obvious Jewish writers, to include popular novelists such as Dennis Wheatley and H.G. Wells. No *The Devil Rides Out* or *The War of the Worlds* in the libraries of Nazi Britain.

We have been educated by the movies into believing that Britain would heroically resist to the last man, woman or child. The reality would probably have been something similar to the case in Norway: a small amount of active collaboration by pro-Nazis, a certain degree of resistance (followed by consequent massive retaliation, such as the execution of civilian hostages chosen at random), and the majority of people just trying to get enough to eat and keep their families safe. The policy of Germany throughout occupied Europe was to rule through the existing institutions, and so the local town hall and police force would, however reluctantly, have become arms of the Nazi state. The key to obedience was not just that the Nazis had the monopoly on violence – and the willingness to use it to a truly sickening degree – but that they had an even greater means of coercion: the threat of deportation.

Liverpool, where the Nazis planned to set up office.
(LOC, LC-DIG-ppmsc-08555)

The occupation plans stated that, after British industry had been stripped of anything useful, all able-bodied men would be deported to work as forced labourers in the Fatherland. In practice this would have meant relocating some 11 million men, around one quarter of the total population. The birth rate would have plummeted to an unsustainable degree, and within a generation the population would be heading for extinction – unless, that is, British women took Germans as husbands en masse. In reality it would have been unwise to deport all the men – who would mine the coal and run the power stations? – but it could have been used on a local basis, say as retribution for acts of resistance. In the Channel Islands, occupied since 1940, some 4 per cent of the population was deported, but the threat of instant mass deportation hung over everyone, and so the only acts of resistance were symbolic – chalking V for Victory on gateposts, for example – rather than active and violent.

The Gestapo in the town halls; police stations turned into SS torture chambers; and a country economically despoiled to the last silver sixpence. No wonder we have good reason to be grateful to 'The Few' and all the others who kept Hitler at bay in 1940.

BIBLIOGRAPHY

Ackroyd, Peter, *Tudors: The History of England, Volume 2* (London: Pan MacMillan, 2012)

Allason-Jones, Lindsay, *Women in Roman Britain* (London: British Museum, 1989)

Alderman, Clifford Lindsey, *Blood-Red the Roses: the Wars of the Roses* (Folkestone: Bailey Brothers and Swinfen, 1973)

Ashdown, Dulcie A., *Royal Murders: Hatred, Revenge and the Seizing of Power* (Stroud: Sutton Publishing, 1998)

Babington, Anthony, *Military Intervention in Britain: from the Gordon Riots to the Gibraltar Incident* (London: Routledge, 1990)

Bagley, J.J., *Historical Interpretation 1: Sources of English Medieval History, 1066-1540* (Harmondsworth: Penguin, 1971)

Banks, Arthur, *A Military Atlas of the First World War* (London: Leo Cooper, 1989)

Barlow, Frank, *William Rufus* (Berkeley and Los Angeles: University of California Press, 1983)

Barrow, Geoffrey W.S., *Robert Bruce & The Community of the Realm of Scotland* (Edinburgh: Edinburgh University Press, 1988 [1965])

Bartlett, Robert, *England Under the Norman and Angevin Kings 1075-1225* (Oxford: Oxford University Press, 2000)

Bates, David, *William the Conqueror* (London: George Philip, 1989)

Bello S.M., Parfitt S.A., & Stringer C.B., 'Earliest Directly-Dated Human Skull-Cups' in *PLoS ONE* 6(2), 2011

Bennett, Martyn, *The Civil Wars 1637-1653* (Stroud: Sutton Publishing, 1998)

Bingham, Caroline, *The Life and Times of Edward II* (London: Book Club Associates, 1973)

Brent, Peter, *The Viking Saga* (London: Book Club Associates, 1975)

Brewer, Clifford, *The Death of Kings: A Medical History of the Kings and Queens of England* (London: Abson Books, 2000)

Brooke, Christopher, *From Alfred to Henry III 871–1272* (London: Sphere, 1969)

Brothwell, Don, *The Bog Man and the Archaeology of People* (London: British Museum, 1986)

Cantor, Norman F. (ed.), *The Pimlico Encyclopedia of the Middle Ages* (London: Pimlico, 1999)

Carman, John (ed.), *Material Harm: Archaeological Studies of War and Violence* (Glasgow: Cruithne Press, 1997)

Carman, John & Anthony Harding (eds), *Ancient Warfare* (Stroud: Sutton Publishing, 1999)

Christensen, Jonas, "Warfare in the European Neolithic" in *Acta Archaeologica*, Vol. 75, 2004

Connolly, S.J. (ed.), *The Oxford Companion to Irish History* (Oxford: Oxford University Press, 1998)

Crossley-Holland, Kevin, *The Anglo-Saxon World: An Anthology* (Oxford: Oxford University Press, 1999)

Daniell, Christopher, *Death and Burial in Medieval England: 1066–1550* (London and New York: Routledge, 1997)

Earle, Peter, *The Life and Times of Henry V* (London: Book Club Associates, 1972)

Fido, Martin, *A History of British Serial Killing* (London: Mortimer/Carlton, 2005)

Fido, Martin, & Keith Skinner, *The Official Encyclopedia of Scotland Yard* (London: Virgin, 1999)

Freeman, Jessica, 'Sorcery at Court and Manor: Margery Jourdemayne, the Witch of Eye next Westminster' in *Journal of Medieval History*, Vol. 30, 2004

Gillingham, John, *The Life and Times of Richard I* (London: Book Club Associates, 1973)

Glover, Richard A., *Britain at Bay: Defence against Bonaparte, 1803-14* (London: George Allen & Unwin, 1973)

Gottfried, Robert S., *The Black Death: Natural and Human Disaster in Medieval Europe* (London: Robert Hale, 1983)

Grinnell-Milne, Duncan, *The Killing of William Rufus* (Newton Abbott: David & Charles, 1968)

Hallam, Elizabeth (ed.), *Chronicles of the Age of Chivalry* (London: Guild Publishing, 1987)

Hanson, Neil, *The Confident Hope of a Miracle: The True History of the Spanish Armada* (London: Random House, 2011)

Harvey, John, *The Plantagenets* (Glasgow: Fontana/Collins, 1981)

Haywood, John, *Encyclopaedia of the Viking Age* (London: Thames & Hudson, 2000)

Hewison, W.S., *Scapa Flow in War and Peace* (Kirkwall: Bellavista Publications, 1995)

Hibbert, Christopher, *The English: A Social History 1066–1945* (London: Paladin/Grafton, 1987)

Hibbert, Christopher, *Queen Victoria: A Personal History* (London: HarperCollins, 2000)

Hoffmann, Ann, *Lives of the Tudor Age 1485–1603* (London: Osprey, 1977)

Hogge, Alice, *God's Secret Agents: Queen Elizabeth's Forbidden Priests and the Hatching of the Gunpowder Plot* (London: Harper Perennial, 2006)

Horspool, David, *Why Alfred Burned the Cakes: A king and his eleven-hundred-year afterlife* (London: Profile Books, 2006)

Howarth, David, *The Men-of-War* (Amsterdam: Time-Life Books, 1980)

Jacob, E.F., *The Fifteenth Century 1399-1485* (Oxford: Oxford University Press, 1985)

Jones, Gwyn, *A History of the Vikings* (Oxford: Oxford University Press, 1973)

Kapelle, William E., *The Norman Conquest of the North: the region and its transformation, 1000–1135* (University of North Carolina Press; Chapel Hill, 1979)

Keeley, Lawrence H., *War Before Civilization: The Myth of the Peaceful Savage* (Oxford: Oxford University Press, 1996)

Keys, David, 'A Viking Mystery' in *Smithsonian* magazine, October 2010

Klingaman, William, *The First Century: Emperors, Gods and Everyman* (London: Hamish Hamilton, 1991)

Lacey, Brian, *The Siege of Derry* (Dublin: Derry City Council/Eason & Son, 1989)

Lacey, Brian, *Discover Derry* (Dublin: The O'Brien Press, 1999)

Lane, Brian, *The Encyclopedia of Cruel and Unusual Punishment* (London: True Crime/Virgin, 1993)

Longmate, Norman, *Defending the Island* (London: Hutchison, 1983)

Longmate, Norman, *If Britain Had Fallen* (London: Greenhill Books, 2004)

Lucy, Sam and Andrew Reynolds (eds), *Burial in Early Medieval England and Wales* (London: The Society for Medieval Archaeology, 2002)

McKisack, May, *The Fourteenth Century 1307–1399* (Oxford: Oxford University Press, 1985)

McLynn, Frank J., *Invasion: From the Armada to Hitler, 1588–1945* (Oxford: Routledge & Keegan Paul, 1987)

Marshall, Rosalind K., *Mary I* (London: HMSO, 1993)

Martin, Colin & Geoffrey Parker, *The Spanish Armada* (Manchester: Manchester University Press, 1999)

Mattingly, Garrett, *The Defeat of the Spanish Armada* (London: Penguin, 1988)

Moffatt, Alistair, *The Wall: Rome's Greatest Frontier* (Edinburgh: Birlinn, 2008)

Morgan, Prys & David Thomas, *Wales: The Shaping of a Nation* (Newton Abbot: David & Charles, 1984)

Muir, Richard, *The National Trust Guide to Dark Age and Medieval Britain 400–1350* (London: George Philip, 1985)

Murphy, Paul Thomas, *Shooting Victoria: Madness, Mayhem, and the Rebirth of the British Monarchy* (London: Head of Zeus, 2012)

Newark, Tim, *Women Warlords: an illustrated military history of female warriors* (London: Blandford, 1989)

Paine, Lincoln P., *Warships of the World to 1900* (Boston & New York: Houghton Mifflin Harcourt, 2000)

Pennisi, Elizabeth, 'Cannibalism and Prion Disease May Have Been Rampant in Ancient Humans' in *Science*, Vol. 300 no. 5617, 11 April 2003

Pollard, Justin, *Seven Ages of Britain* (London: Hodder & Stoughton, 2003)

Poole, A.L., *Domesday to Magna Carta 1087–1216* (Oxford: Oxford University Press, 1985)

Porter, Stephen, *The Great Fire of London* (Stroud: Sutton Publishing, 1996)

Powicke, Maurice, *The Thirteenth Century 1216–1307* (Oxford: Oxford University Press, 1985)

Prescott, H.F.M., *Mary Tudor: The Spanish Tudor* (London: Phoenix, 2003 [1940])

Purkiss, Diane, *The English Civil War: A People's History* (London: HarperPress, 2006)

Ramsey, Winston G., *The War in the Channel Islands, Then and Now* (London: Battle of Britain Prints International, 1981)

Rogozinski, Jan, *Pirates!* (New York: Facts on File, 1995)

Roesdahl, Else, *The Vikings* (London: Allen Lane/Penguin, 1991)

Ross, Josephine, *The Tudors* (London: Artus, 1979)

Rumbelow, Donald, *The Complete Jack the Ripper* (London: Penguin, 1988)

Rumbelow, Donald, *The Houndsditch Murders and the Siege of Sidney Street* (Stroud: The History Press, 2008)

Savage, Anne (ed. & trans.), *The Anglo-Saxon Chronicles* (Godalming: CLB Publishing, 1995)

Sawyer, Peter (ed.), *The Oxford Illustrated History of the Vikings* (Oxford: Oxford University Press, 1997)

Schama, Simon, *A History of Britain* 3 Vols. (London: BBC Worldwide, 2000)

Simons, Eric N., *The Devil in the Vault: A Life of Guy Fawkes* (London: Frederick Muller, 1963)

Smith, Lacy Baldwin, *The Horizon Book of the Elizabethan World* (London: Paul Hamlyn, 1967)

Smurthwaite, David, *The Complete Guide to the Battlefields of Britain* (Harmondsworth: Michael Joseph/Penguin, 1993)

Stenton, Frank, *Anglo-Saxon England* (Oxford: Oxford University Press, 1989)

Tait, Charles, *The Orkney Guide Book* (Orkney: Charles Tait Photographic, 1997)

Taylor, Timothy, 'The Edible Dead' in *British Archaeology*, No.59, June 2001

Times, John, *The Romance of London: Strange Stories, Scenes and Remarkable Persons of the Great Town* (London: Frederick Warne & Co., 1901)

Todd, Malcolm (ed.), *A Companion to Roman Britain* (Oxford: John Wiley & Sons, 2008)

Vallance, Edward, *A Radical History of Britain* (London: Little, Brown, 2009)

Vaughan-Thomas, Wynford, *The Splendour Falls* (Cardiff and Llandybie: HTV Cymru/Wales & Christopher Davies, 1973)

Wacher, John, *Roman Britain* (Stroud: Sutton Publishing, 2001)

Warner, Philip, *Invasion Road* (London: Cassell, 1980)

Warner, Philip, *World War One: A Narrative* (London: Cassell, 1998)

Warren, W.L., *King John* (London: Book Club Associates, 1974)

Webster, Graham, *The Roman Invasion of Britain* (London: B.T. Batsford, 1993)

Wharam, Alan, *Treason: Famous English Treason Trials* (Stroud: Alan Sutton, 1995)

Williams, Neville, *The Life and Times of Elizabeth I* (London: Book Club Associates, 1972)